OPENING CRED

A Word from the Editing Room.. 2

Remembering Angela Lansbury.. 3

In Memoriam.. 4

And Hell Followed With Him... Pale Rider by James Lecky................ 5

Mannequin by Simon J. Ballard.. 10

High Road to Stardom - Tom Selleck's '80s Movies by Jonathon Dabell.. 14

Warren Beatty's Masterpiece - Reds by John H. Foote...................... 23

White Dog by Steven West.. 28

Give My Regards to Broad Street by Stephen Mosley........................ 33

The Funhouse - An Underrated Thrill Ride by David Flack.................. 36

The Amateur by Joe Secrett.. 40

Ladyhawke by Darren Linder.. 43

Harold's Long, No Good, Very Bad Day - The Long Good Friday by Rachel Bellwoar.. 48

"It's All in the Reflexes" - Big Trouble in Little China by Peter Sawford.. 51

'80s Christmas Cheer by Nic Parker.. 56

Agnes of God by Dr. Andrew C. Webber.. 65

Screwballs, Joysticks and Cherry Forever - Taking a Dirty Peek at the 1980s American Teen Sex Comedies by John Harrison.................. 69

Tough Guys Don't Dance by Aaron Stielstra.................................. 81

The Three Great Sci-fi Remakes of the '80s by James Aaron.............. 86

Contemporary Cowboys of the '80s - Lone Wolf McQuade and Extreme Prejudice by Ian Taylor.. 93

Caricatures by Aaron Stielstra.. 98

Closing Credits.. 99

Contributors this issue: James Aaron, Simon J. Ballard, Rachel Bellwoar, Jonathon Dabell, David Flack, John H. Foote, John Harrison, James Lecky, Darren Linder, Stephen Mosley, Nic Parker, Peter Sawford, Joe Secrett, Aaron Stielstra, Ian Taylor, Dr Andrew C. Webber, Steven West. Caricature artwork by Aaron Stielstra.

All articles, photographs and specially produced artwork remain copyright their respective author/photographer/artist. Opinions expressed herein are those of the individual.

Design and Layout: Dawn Dabell
Copy Editor: Jonathon Dabell

Most images in this magazine come from the private collection of Dawn and Jonathon Dabell, or the writer of the corresponding article. Those which do not are made available in an effort to advance understanding of cultural issues pertaining to academic research. We believe this constitutes 'fair use' of any such copyrighted material as provided for in Section 107 of the US Copyright Law. In accordance with Title U.S.C Section 107, this magazine is sold to those who have expressed a prior interest in receiving the included information for research, academic and educational purposes.

Printed globally by Amazon KDP

A Word from the Editing Room

Greetings, readers!

Welcome to Issue 2 of 'Cinema of the '80s'. If you're returning after enjoying Issue 1, it's great to have you back. If you're discovering us for the first time, we're delighted to have you aboard!

In our latest edition, we're thrilled to offer a great assortment of articles for your reading pleasure. But first, we need to welcome two new writers to our fold. James Aaron hails from Kentucky in the United States and is responsible for an excellent piece about three major sci-fi remakes which hit the screens during the '80s - *The Thing*, *The Fly* and *The Blob*. Meanwhile, Nic Parker from Germany takes a look at six classic Christmas movies from the decade (well, five plus *Planes, Trains & Automobiles*, which is a Thanksgiving movie if we're being pedantic but festive enough to deserve its pl;ace). Several contributors from our sister publication, 'Cinema of the '70s' magazine, are also making their first appearance in this '80s-themed spin-off.

Among the content served up for your enjoyment is an analysis of *Pale Rider*, a deep dive into the teen sex comedies of the decade, a look at the contemporary westerns *Lone Wolf McQuade* and *Extreme Prejudice*, an examination of *Ladyhawke* and a review of T*he Long Good Friday*. Plus much, much more, of course! Flick back to the contents page for the full list.

As is always the case, it's been a real pleasure putting together this edition of the magazine. Our team comprises a mix of professional authors and enthusiastic amateurs, and we're bowled over every time by their collective insight, passion, knowledge and enthusiasm. We hope and trust those qualities shine through and that you, our valued readers, come away from every article entertained and enlightened. Thanks once again for your continued support, and we'll see you in a few months for Issue 3!

Dawn and Jonathon Dabell

Remembering Angela Lansbury (1925-2022)

On October 11th, 2022, Angela Lansbury died at the age of 96. She was five days short of her 97th birthday. As one of the last remaining stars of the Golden Age of Hollywood, she had been active in the industry since the 1940s and was still making movies at the point of her passing, her final role being a brief posthumous appearance in *Glass Onion: A Knives Out Mystery* (2022). In the '80s, she was offered two potentially huge television projects - one a sitcom, one a detective series. Her agent advised her to take the sitcom, but Lansbury opted for the detective show. It proved a wise choice - *Murder, She Wrote* ran for 12 years and encompassed 264 episodes. It was one of the most successful TV shows of all time.

Her '80s films were:

The Mirror Crack'd (1980)

The Last Unicorn (1982)

Sweeney Todd: The Demon Barber of Fleet Street (TV movie) (1982)

The Pirates of Penzance (1983)

The Gift of Love: A Christmas Story (TV movie) (1983)

A Talent for Murder (TV movie) (1984)

The Company of Wolves (1984)

Rage of Angels: The Story Continues (TV movie) (1986)

Shootdown (TV movie) (1988)

The Shell Seekers (TV movie) (1989)

Farewell, Miss Lansbury. Thanks for the memories.

In Memoriam

**Kirstie Alley
(1951-2022)**
Actress, known for *Star Trek II: The Wrath of Khan* (1982) and *Look Who's Talking* (1989).

**Louise Fletcher
(1934-2022)**
Actress, known for *Invaders from Mars* (1986) and *Flowers in the Attic* (1987).

**Mike Hodges
(1932-2022)**
Director, known for *Flash Gordon* (1980) and *A Prayer for the Dying* (1987).

**Stuart Margolin
(1940-2022)**
Actor, known for *Class* (1983) and *Iron Eagle II* (1988).

**Olivia Newton-John
(1948-2022)**
Actress, known for *Xanadu* (1980) and *Two of a Kind* (1983).

**Irene Papas
(1929-2022)**
Actress, known for *Lion of the Desert* (1981) and *The Assisi Underground* (1985).

**Wolfgang Petersen
(1941-2022)**
Director, known for *Das Boot* (1981) and *The Neverending Story* (1984).

**Albert Pyun
(1953-2022)**
Director, known for *The Sword and the Sorcerer* (1982) and *Cyborg* (1989).

**Bob Rafelson
(1933-2022)**
Director, known for *The Postman Always Rings Twice* (1981) and *Mountains of the Moon* (1989).

**Henry Silva
(1926-2022)**
Actor, known for *Sharky's Machine* (1981) and *Code of Silence* (1985).

And Hell Followed with Him...

PALE RIDER

by James Lecky

Carbon Canyon, California. A group of tin-pan miners eke out a precarious living searching for gold. But the local land baron Coy LaHood (Richard Dysart), who uses much more intensive and destructive mining methods, is determined to drive them out by any means necessary, including intimidation and violence.

In the aftermath of an attack on the settlement, a young girl named Megan (Sydney Penny) prays for a miracle - and one arrives in the shape of the mysterious Preacher (Clint Eastwood), a man of God who is handy with both his fists and pistols. In response, LaHood employs Marshal Stockburn (John Russell) and his gang of deputies to enforce his will. The scene is set for a brutal showdown.

Although closely associated with the genre, Eastwood has appeared in relatively few westerns. Discounting his television work, a couple of early oaters in which he played supporting roles, the musical *Paint Your Wagon* (1969) and Don Siegel's gothic melodrama *The Beguiled* (1971), Eastwood has appeared in only ten westerns - four of which he directed - in a career spanning some sixty-odd feature films.

On the other hand, of course, his westerns rank among some of the most important ever made. The success

of *A Fistful of Dollars* (1964) changed the genre visually, psychologically and musically. Leone's subsequent films with Eastwood (*For a Few Dollars More* [1965] and *The Good, The Bad and the Ugly* [1966]) not only brought the term 'spaghetti western' into the mainstream, legitimising the hitherto ridiculous notion of the European western, they also helped define and refine Eastwood's on-screen persona, which took its impetus from John Wayne's "talk low, talk slow and don't talk too much" school of acting, alongside a screen style reminiscent of Gary Cooper and Toshiro Mifune.

The western genre is practically as old as cinema itself. Edwin S. Porter's *The Great Train Robbery* was produced in 1903 and even before that, the pioneering Mitchell and Kenyon - based in Blackburn, Lancashire - had made *Kidnapping by Indians* (1899). The genre remained popular for many years, and even unlikely stars like Errol Flynn (*Dodge City* [1939] and *They Died with Their Boots* On [1941]), and James Cagney and Humphrey Bogart (co-stars in *The Oklahoma Kid* [1939]) were drawn into its orbit.

Broadly, the western might be divided into three periods: Classic, European and Revisionist.

The Classic period is best exemplified by John Ford, replete with notions of Manifest Destiny and Taming a Lawless Land - *My Darling Clementine* (1946) and *She Wore a Yellow Ribbon* (1949) - although by the '50s such directors as Anthony Mann, Robert Aldrich and Budd Boetticher had begun to chip away at the old certainties.

Leone ushered in a new era when all eyes turned to Europe. Some six hundred westerns were made there between the early '60s and late '70s. The lawman gave way to the gunfighter (or, often, the bounty hunter) and the main inspiration came not from history (or its interpretation) but from the cinematic western itself.

Thereafter came the Revisionist period during which the western - in particular the American western - attempted to depict a more realistic vision of the West with such films as *Bad Company* (1972), *Dirty Little Billy* (1972) and, perhaps most notably, *The Culpepper Cattle Company* (1972). With its glamour shorn, the western did not live long as a popular form, and while there are those who point to Michael Cimino's *Heaven's Gate* (1980) as its death knell, the reality is that the genre had long been in decline.

Pale Rider (1985) was Eastwood's response to the Classic period and, perhaps tellingly, it became the most successful western of the '80s.

Prior to this, Eastwood had travelled the road laid down by the Man with No Name (a construct of Hollywood marketing). His characters were motivated by either *profit* (Joe/Manco/Blondie in the Leone films; Hogan in *Two Mules for Sister Sarah* [1970]) or *revenge* (Jed Cooper in *Hang 'em High* [1968]; the titular stranger in *High Plain's Drifter* [1973]; or Josey Wales in Eastwood's masterpiece *The Outlaw Josey Wales* [1976]). But with *Pale Rider*, Eastwood plays a variation on his screen image.

For once, he is authentically the hero. *Justice* is his motivation (although, significantly, not the kind of justice dealt out by Harry Callahan in *Dirty Harry* (1971). Compare and contrast

Preacher's arrival with that of the Man with No Name in *A Fistful of Dollars*. Upon reaching San Miguel, TMWNN sees a young boy being beaten and shot at, but does nothing other than observe. However, when the Preacher sees Hull Barret (Michael Moriarty) being attacked by LaHood's men, he immediately comes to his rescue, wielding an axe-handle ("Nothing like a nice piece of hickory") before escorting Hull home.

There, he meets the other settlers of Carbon Canyon and, more importantly, Hull's 'intended' Sarah Wheeler (Carrie Snodgress) and her daughter Megan, and reveals himself to be a Man of the Cloth.

While he and Hull are attempting to shatter a particularly stubborn boulder which Hull believes is concealing a deposit of gold, LaHood's son Joshua (Chris Penn) arrives accompanied by the hulking Club (Richard Kiel). Their aim is to attempt to scare the Preacher away. Needless to say, it doesn't succeed, and in one of the film's few comical moments, Club is taken down with two blows from a sledgehammer - one to the face, another to the groin - then gently helped back on his horse ("put 'em in a little ice, that'll take care of it.")

The film's most obvious touchstone is George Stevens' *Shane* (1953). The overall plot - tenacious settlers embattled by a greedy land baron - and certain scenes (the breaking of the boulder; the death of Spider Conway [Doug McGrath] after being shot down in the street by Stockburn; and the final frames with Megan calling after the departing Preacher) have a strong echo of Stevens' film.

Equally, there are other influences at work here. The 'stalk and shoot' ending recalls *High Noon* (1952) or, for that matter, similar sequences in Leone's *The Good, the Bad and the Ugly* and *Once Upon a Time in the West* (1968). The destruction of LaHood's mining operation might be seen as a tip of the hat to the dynamite throwing climax of *Rio Bravo* (1959). The Preacher deals with Club in much the same way that Butch deals with Harvey Logan in *Butch Cassidy and the Sundance Kid* (1969). And the stunning cinematography of Bruce Surtees (in his last collaboration with Eastwood) recalls William Mellor's work on *The Naked Spur* (1953), with which *Pale Rider* shares a love of landscape.

There is another little nod to Leone with the death of Coy LaHood, shot by Hull as he tries to drygulch the Preacher, a moment that owes much to the death of Esteban Rojo in *A Fistful of Dollars*, killed by Silvanito while attempting to shoot Joe in the back.

This is not to say, however, that *Pale Rider* is a patchwork of homages to westerns past. Rather, it is one which understands and celebrates the form.

In some ways, all genre writing is an engagement with itself - the tropes and forms of, say, science fiction are common currency, as are those of the thriller, horror,

war and, of course, the western genres. When it comes to genre, there is little that is startlingly new. Even when Leone breathed new life into the western, he did so by standing on the shoulders of others (perhaps most notably Akira Kurosawa and Budd Boetticher). Eastwood's Oscar-winning *Unforgiven* (1992) made the link between past and present explicit by dedicating itself "To Sergio and Don."

As ever in his westerns, Eastwood draws upon a strong supporting cast. During the '70s, he assembled what might be thought of as a stock company for his films, actors like Bill McKinney, Woodrow Parfrey, William O'Connell and Geoffrey Lewis who would work with him many times, often in unsympathetic roles. *Pale Rider* has few of these familiar faces, though it does feature Doug McGrath and John Russell, both memorable as the odious Lige and Bloody Bill respectively in *The Outlaw Josey Wales*. Among the newcomers (e.g. non-stock company) are the likes of Dysart, Penn, Kiel, Snodgress, Penny and Moriarty. Veteran actor Dysart is perfectly cast as LaHood, a land baron in the same mould as Rufus Ryker from *Shane* or Nathan Burdett from *Rio Bravo* (coincidentally played by John Russell). Like all the best villains, he is utterly convinced that he is right. LaHood uses hydraulic mining to strip the land away, regardless of the resulting destruction, a brutal contrast with the peaceful miners who gently and patiently pan the riverbeds for nuggets.

Penn brings an edgy nervousness to Joshua LaHood, a wannabe tough guy. He would reappear in the guise of Nice Guy Eddie in Tarantino's *Reservoir Dogs* (1992). Kiel, of course, achieved his greatest fame as Jaws in the James Bond films *The Spy Who Loved Me* (1977) and *Moonraker* (1979), both directed by Lewis Gilbert.

Snodgress was an award-winning actor who appeared in both film and television, including Brian De Palma's *The Fury* (1978) as well as guest appearances in *Quincy M.E*, *The X-Files* and *The West Wing*. Sarah's attraction to the Preacher is low-key but powerful, expressed in a single on-screen kiss while the word "Preacher" - seemingly spoken by Stockburn - echoes through the hills. Yet, in the great western tradition, the implication of the line "close the door" hints at something else.

Pale Rider remains Penny's most recognisable screen performance, but her career continues to span a wide range of television productions, including a stint in the long-running soap *The Bold and the Beautiful*. As Megan, she is fragile, vulnerable and naïve and, like Sarah, very much taken with the fantasy rather than the reality of the Preacher.

Further down the list is a young hawk-faced Billy Drago,

playing one of Stockburn's deputies. He was memorable as Frank Nitti in De Palma's *The Untouchables* (1987), and thereafter appeared in many straight-to-video productions of varying quality.

But the real casting coup in *Pale Rider* is Moriarty as Hull Barret. Throughout the '80s in particular, he brought a certain gravitas to such Larry Cohen films as *Q: The Winged Serpent* (1982), *The Stuff* (1985), *It's Alive III: Island of the Alive* (1987) and *A Return to Salem's Lot* (1987). Hull Barret - much like Joe Starrett in *Shane* - is the archetypal 'Good Man' who tries to hold his community together and strives to do what is right. Deeply in love with Sarah, he is a somewhat resented father figure to Megan and an unlikely, if perfect, foil to the Preacher.

Eastwood, of course, sits at the heart of it all: mysterious and practically monolithic. By this stage in his career, he could - and would continue to - surround himself with the best talent possible both in front of and behind the camera.

The Preacher differs from his other western personas,

...and hell followed with him.

CLINT EASTWOOD
PALE RIDER

CLINT EASTWOOD "PALE RIDER" also starring MICHAEL MORIARTY CARRIE SNODGRESS CHRISTOPHER PENN RICHARD DYSART SYDNEY PENNY RICHARD KIEL DOUG McGRATH JOHN RUSSELL executive producer FRITZ MANES music by LENNIE NIEHAUS associate producer DAVID VALDES written by MICHAEL BUTLER & DENNIS SHRYACK produced and directed by CLINT EASTWOOD A WARNER COMMUNICATIONS COMPANY

but only in certain ways - a little more compassionate, less swift to use his gun. Regardless, this is still the Eastwood of the cool quip and the fast pistol, a little older now, but more than capable of the sort of slaughter he deals out at the end to LaHood's men and Stockburn's deputies, and indeed Stockburn himself (killed in that most recognisable of western tropes - the showdown in the street).

Like the protagonist of *High Plains Drifter*, the Preacher has a supernatural aspect about him. The suggestion is strong that he is an avenging spirit conjured up by Megan's fervent prayer. The scars on his back, a grouping of bullet-holes and the fact Stockburn appears to recall him ("The man I'm thinking about is dead") add weight to the theory, as does the Preacher's statement: "It's an old score; it's time to settle it". But the truth is ambiguous, up to the viewer to decide. The semi-supernatural or reincarnated/reborn gunfighter had appeared on occasion in Italian westerns - *Django Kill...* (1967), *Requiescant* (1967), *If You Meet Sartana. . . Pray for Your Death* (1968), *The Stranger's Gundown* (aka *Django the Bastard*) (1969) - and the Preacher could easily belong among them.

In addition, *Pale Rider* has often been referred to as an eco-western and certainly Eastwood's eye for landscape and, in particular, the devastating effects of hydraulic mining upon it, would suggest an underlying concern. The destruction of LaHood's operation towards the end of the film is a stark statement. The Preacher does not simply protect the settlers but brings utter ruin down on LaHood. And hell followed with him, indeed (a reference to the Four Horsemen of the Apocalypse in the Book of Revelation, with Eastwood cast as Death)

The low-key soundtrack by Lennie Niehaus is a perfect accompaniment for the film - lush in places, spare in others - and the screenplay, by Dennis Shyrack and Michael Butler, is intelligent and beautifully paced. The pair had previously provided the screenplay for *The Gauntlet* (1977) whereas Niehaus, who had scored such Eastwood films as *Tightrope* (1984), would work with him again on *Heartbreak Ridge* (1986), *Unforgiven* and *The Bridges of Madison County* (1995), among others.

Pale Rider headed a mini resurgence in the genre's fortunes, paving the way for films such as *Silverado* (1985), *Young Guns* (1988), the television epic *Lonesome Dove* (1989), the Oscar-winning *Dances with Wolves* (1990) and, of course, Eastwood's western swansong, *Unforgiven*.

When *Pale Rider* was released, Eastwood was not quite the acclaimed filmmaker he would become. He was still seen in some ways as just a purveyor of slam-bang entertainment. But it remains an important milestone in his development, and proof that there was still life in the western.

Mannequin

When she comes to life anything can happen!

by **Simon J. Ballard**

Not many romantic comedies begin in Dfu, Egypt, around 2000 B.C, or "A really long time ago, right before lunch" as an onscreen caption informs us, borrowing a visual gag from *Monty Python's Life of Brian*. In a modestly assembled tomb, we are introduced to Ema Hesire (Kim Cattrall) who, we quickly learn, has no desire to be married off by her mother to a fuel merchant (or camel dung dealer, to be precise). Her plea for help from the gods seems to have been granted when she disappears in a flash of lightning and a whoosh of smoke. She is reincarnated, after a trip through the ages, as that most inanimate of objects - a shop window mannequin.

Director and co-writer Michael Gottlieb formed the idea for *Mannequin* (1987) when he spied what he thought was a moving dummy in a store window whilst walking along Manhattan's Fifth Avenue. It turned out to be a trick of the light, but the production company Gladden Entertainment - in association with 20th Century Fox - still felt the idea of a mannequin coming to life might lend itself to a fun and appealing movie. The concept bears some relation to the 1948 production *One Touch of Venus*, in which a window dresser kisses a Venus statue and causes it to turn into a very-much alive Ava Gardner, though Gottlieb didn't acknowledge whether this was an inspiration. One could find possible influences too in the 'Pygmalion' story, or even an episode of Hammer's 1968 TV anthology show *Journey to the Unknown* called *Eve*, in which Dennis Waterman falls in love with an animated dummy.

This film is what I would call a guilty pleasure. I'm well aware that it has been critically trounced through the years, and I will admit it has plenty of flaws. I'll even admit that, as a comedy, it doesn't boast a particularly good script on the whole. There just aren't enough decent gags, for one thing. There is, however, a bucket load of the feel-good factor which I find constantly irresistible. And although the concept is not especially original, it is different and enjoyable enough to be extremely appealing.

Now, I'm a fan of Richard Curtis' saccharine sweet romantic comedies, but I find *Mannequin* has a little more diversity on show and that's refreshing for an '80s film of this type. Much of that comes from female lead Kim Cattrall herself. In a Hollywood age where beauty equated to youth, female stars were generally considered 'past it' once they were beyond their twenties. How nice it is, therefore, to have Cattrall at 30 sparring off McCarthy, then aged 24. This kind of age gap, while not huge, was mainly considered a big no-no back then.

I should also single out the black actor Meschach Taylor who plays a very camp, flamboyant and happily 'out' gay character named Hollywood Montrose. There are no subtleties here and, although the character is played by a heterosexual actor, I can say - as a gay man myself - that I've met many people like Hollywood Montrose in real life. Just having the actor in the picture, playing such a self-assured character, is a welcome inclusion.

So, the plot. Well, it seems the gods have allowed the artistic life drifter Jonathan Switcher (Andrew McCarthy) to sculpt Ema, or Emmy as she likes to be called, into a shop-window mannequin. However, his obsession with perfection gets him fired from the manufacturers, leading him to take on a variety of ill-fated jobs which we witness in a breezy montage accompanied by Sylvester Levay's optimistic soundtrack. Switcher takes on the job of a balloon wrangler but the birthday boy takes off into the air at his own party; a landscape gardener, fired for sculpting a giant bunny out of a hedge; and a pizza chef, given the boot after taking too much time arranging the toppings to suit his own aesthetic.

After saving the life of Prince & Co. department store owner Mrs. Timkin (the wonderous Estelle Getty) in a sequence worthy of Buster Keaton, Switcher finds himself hired as a warehouse attendant. It is here he meets Emmy, a mannequin who happens to be the reincarnation of Ema from the opening scene. Moreover, we soon discover she can come to life in front of him alone. McCarthy and Cattrall spark off each other well, engaging in a warm chemistry that basically forms much of what I love about this movie. His initial bewilderment, coupled with her fascination for 20th century machine tools, makes for enjoyable viewing, even if it leads to her nearly spearing him in the head with a nail gun!

There are a number of obstacles which threaten Switcher's new-found attraction for the 4,501-year-old Egyptian. Obstacle number one is James Spader, playing against type as Prince & Co.'s manager Mr. Richards, hair gelled flat against his head like wet cement as he creeps and crawls obsequiously around Mrs. Timkin. He engages in industrial espionage with rival store Illustra's head honcho B.J. Wert (played with patronising menace by Steve Vinovich). Obstacle number two is the hilarious (or irritating, depending on your point of view) G.W. Bailey as Prince and Co.'s security guard, Captain Felix Maxwell. Essentially, Bailey here reprises his *Police Academy* bit, using bluster and bumptiousness to mask his basic imbecility. The film reunites him with his co-star from the original *Police Academy* film, Kim Cattrall. Obstacle

three is Switcher's aspirational soon-to-be ex-girlfriend Roxie Shields (a deliciously bitchy turn from Carole Davis) who is Illustra's woman on the inside, attempting to lure her former lover into the fold. *Dynasty* material, if ever I saw it.

Richards hopes to persuade Mrs. Timkin to sell the ailing store to Illustra but his plan is dashed when Emmy creates crowd-pleasing windows which Jonathan takes credit for. Whether they're sporty displays with revolving tennis racquets or bicycles 'moving' against a rolling backcloth, they push the store's profits up and Switcher is promoted to Visual Merchandiser then finally Vice President. And all the while, with Emmy staying perfectly still in front of others, their love blossoms in secret and the music plays.

The opening animated titles, produced by Sally Cruikshank, shows Emmy's trip through time to the accompaniment of Belinda Carlisle's *In My Wildest Dreams*, a spirited and cheerful tune that gets us in the mood from the outset. There is also a montage of Switcher and Emmy having fun in the store's clothing department after hours to Alisha's *Do You Dream About Me?*, a fab '80s song with a disco beat that never fails to get me moving. There's also the matter of a certain Number One chart hit which features prominently, but we'll come to that later.

There is a rather comfortable, some might say smug and affluent, air about the movie. It takes place, after all, right in the heart of the yuppie era with people wearing suit jackets with the sleeves rolled up, and the premise itself involves rather a lot of consumerism and soaring profit margins. Scratch the surface, though, and you'll realise that subtle anti-capitalist digs lie within. As Switcher and Emmy lie together in one of the store's hammocks, he dreams of building cities for all, where time is taken to make them as pleasing to the eye as possible rather than the builders trotting out cheap, generic constructions barely worth living in. The world he reacts against is best summed up when Felix, in cahoots with Richards, tries to kidnap Emmy in an attempt to blackmail Switcher into joining Illustra. Breaking into Prince & Co. after having been fired, Felix trains his torch on the mannequins: "You ever notice they all look alike?" he asks Richards. He has no sense of individual beauty or appreciation at all. He is a factory model through and through. It's ironic that Emmy herself is the product of a factory line, albeit one fashioned with unusual personal care and attention thanks to Switcher's artistic dreams.

Switcher's own apartment is rather large, even if it seems to be all one room, but there is a pleasing sense of individuality about it, exemplified by the astrolabe constructed from a stool and a bike wheel. I also love the fact that he wears stolen bowling shoes. This is a man who hates to conform, to be on life's production line, and Emmy is his inspiration despite not being seen by others. McCarthy plays Switcher as a man who wishes he lived in a world less cynical, and he plays the cutely vulnerable type rather well (well, he *is* extremely cute, full stop - there, that's my bit of objectifying over with).

As Emmy, Cattrall gives a delicate performance laced with fragility. As the windows become a huge success, there is a sense of guilt that she is holding Switcher back from his ambitions because of the gods' decree. She plays besotted without being too enthralled, lending an air of non-conformism to the character. You can almost believe this is a woman out of her time, out of step with the modern world yet finding her own niche within it.

As I say, the comedy aspects are generally on the broad side. Armand (Christopher Maher), Roxie's co-worker, offers her a night of "distasteful sex" to get over being snubbed by Switcher, but having made crude single entendres throughout the film, he is ultimately unable to get it up - a flaccid joke in every sense. According to G.W. Bailey, the over-the-top mugging of the supporting cast was very much encouraged by Gottlieb, and he was surprised when *Mannequin* turned out to be a decent box-office hit. There is an entertaining car chase, in which he and Richards hotly pursue Switcher and Emmy on a motorbike. The stunt as their car leaps into the air, only to be trapped in the narrow space between two buildings, is a great visual gag and Spader's outraged expression is to die for.

The climax almost reaches Indiana Jones proportions as a fumingly jealous Roxie dumps Emmy along with a load of other mannequins onto a conveyer belt destined to fall into a rather nasty crusher. It reminds me of the scene in *Indiana Jones and the Temple of Doom* in which a similar conveyor belt heads towards a rock-smashing end, and the characters seem to be on it waaaaaay longer than should be natural!

The gods, it seems, smile upon Emmy. She turns human just as her feet are about to be pulverised in front of the startled janitor. The rest of the world can see their love together! Cue that number one hit as Grace Slick and Mickey Thomas of Starship belt out *Nothing's Gonna Stop Us Now* as - spoiler alert - Switcher and Emmy get married (in the store window, natch). As the credits roll, special mention is made of Phyllis Newman (as Emmy's mum) whose cameo features in the pre-credits scene. A noted singer and actor, Newman was awarded a Tony for the musical *Subways*

Are for Sleeping on Broadway. She is rather gutsy in her small part, and I think it right to single her out for a quick mention.

Watching *Mannequin* again in preparation for this article, I was struck by how inoffensive it is on the whole. Despite being the story of an Egyptian woman reincarnated in the present, it's ultimately a small tale of love against the odds peppered with rousing music and decent performances. It's fluff, yes, I'm happy to admit, but not the type that gets up my nose. I'll leave that sense of irritation for the ill-judged sequel, *Mannequin Two: On the Move*, released in 1991 (and, therefore, out of the range of this magazine). Shame, that. There is only one way to celebrate *Mannequin*, I feel, and that is to put your hands together and give it credit for succeeding in being exactly what it sets out to be.

HIGH ROAD TO STARDOM
TOM SELLECK'S '80S MOVIES

by Jonathon Dabell

There's an interesting reason to examine the '80s big-screen work of Tom Selleck. Mainly, the fact that his career very nearly took an entirely different trajectory after he was screen-tested, then selected, for the role of Indiana Jones in *Raiders of the Lost Ark*. Harrison Ford had auditioned too, but George Lucas (who'd co-written the Indy flick, and whose production company Lucasfilm was heavily involved in making it) didn't want people to get the impression that Ford was his "go-to" man since they'd already collaborated on *American Graffiti*, *Star Wars* and *The Empire Strikes Back*. So Selleck got the nod and was all set to play the whip-cracking, fedora-wearing, adventure-loving archaeologist.

There was one tiny sticking point. Selleck had recently signed a contract to star in a forthcoming TV show *Magnum P.I.*, in which he would play a private eye who solves mysteries and gets up to his neck in adventure in Hawaii. He duly told Lucas and *Raiders* director Steven Spielberg that he was contracted to do the show. They simply smiled and told him not to worry. They didn't foresee any problems getting him released from his commitments. But their confidence in their own clout would turn out to be misplaced.

Selleck was told in no uncertain terms by the producers at CBS that he was doing *Magnum P.I.* No exceptions. No cold feet. No reneging on the agreement. End of story. Thus, he was forced to relinquish the Indy gig and Ford was promptly installed as the character in Selleck's place. Some close to Selleck urged him to do whatever he must to get out of *Magnum*. "Crash your car… Break your

leg… Anything…" But, as the actor explained later, that wasn't his style. He knew he would have to look his family in the eye and admit he had deliberately dishonoured a contract. Either that, or spare them the knowledge by lying to their face. And he wasn't willing to do that, even though the six TV pilots he had so far appeared in had all failed to be picked up and turned into long-running shows.

For many actors, missing the opportunity to play the role of a lifetime might have spelt career oblivion. *Raiders of the Lost Ark* went on to be the highest grossing American movie of its year. The sequel *Indiana Jones and the Temple of Doom* was the second-highest grosser of 1984. The same box-office performance was managed by the third instalment *Indiana Jones and the Last Crusade* in 1989. Selleck could have been part of that box-office juggernaut. Even more galling was the fact that filming the first season of *Magnum P.I.* ended up delayed due to a writers' strike, and it became apparent there *would* have been enough time for him to shoot *Raiders of the Lost Ark* before his Hawaiian-set TV show was ready to roll.

To Selleck's credit, he showed absolute professionalism and gave his all to the role of Thomas Magnum. Largely thanks to him, *Magnum P.I.* became one of the biggest TV shows of all time. It ran from 1980 to 1988 and was nominated for various Golden Globe and Emmy awards, winning quite a few. Selleck himself was nominated multiple times and won both awards at the respective 1984 ceremonies. The character became a household favourite. His loud Hawaiian shirts, red Ferrari and impressive moustache became immediate, identifiable trademarks.

Such was the popularity of *Magnum P.I.* - and, by extension, its lead actor - that big screen opportunities soon beckoned. Selleck had appeared in theatrical movies before, but only in bit parts in the likes of *Myra Breckenridge* (1970), *The Seven Minutes* (1971) and *Coma* (1978). *Raiders of the Lost Ark* would have been his first leading role had it come to fruition. Ultimately, Selleck's first pic as male lead would turn out to be rather similar to an Indy movie - a big period adventure set in central Asia, with spies, guns, bombs, aerial stunts and large-scale battle sequences. The film was *High Road to China* (1983), and as the actor would reflect some years later: "There were actors at that point who had left a series and started a feature career, but there was no-one at that point who was trying to do both at the same time. So that was unique. It also made the jury tough, because a lot of people didn't see it that way, so I was walking into an arena where that wasn't accepted. But it's a good movie. It holds up."

Selleck would make six big-screen movies in the '80s. To this day, there are people who feel he never quite succeeded in transitioning from the small screen, that no matter how many times he tried he couldn't quite replicate his *Magnum* success in a big-budget, feature-length Hollywood production. While it's true that few of Selleck's '80s movies were hits (a couple actually lost money on their initial theatrical run), it should equally be noted that he was top-billed in the highest-grossing US movie of 1987, *Three Men and a Baby*. In fact, all six of his '80s movies have something to offer and, to varying degrees, make for enjoyable viewing. I will now examine them one at a time.

High Road to China (1983)

You'd think *High Road to China* was devised specifically to provide Tom Selleck with the opportunity to star in an Indiana Jones-style adventure film after losing out on the real thing a couple of years earlier. But in reality it is based on a book by Australian author Jon Cleary which was published in 1977, several years before Indiana Jones even existed. The film version wasn't written specifically for Selleck. Roger Moore and Jacqueline Bisset were originally set to star, with John Huston lined up to direct. Huston stepped aside and Sidney J. Furie was named as his replacement; then Bisset pulled out and Bo Derek was offered the vacant female lead, but she was only interested in signing up if her husband John Derek was allowed to direct. Ultimately, it was abandoned.

When the project was revived, Brian G. Hutton (of *Where Eagles Dare* fame) was handed directorial duties and Selleck was cast as a boozy American bi-plane pilot named O'Malley who lives in 1920s Turkey, not far from Istanbul. His hard-drinking ways are the result of some of the horrors he witnessed while flying combat missions during WW1. He is hired by a spunky society heiress, Eve

15

and stutters rather embarrassingly. The film could have done without these scenes. Or, at least, they ought to have been handled differently.

Much better is the glorious aerial photography, the rich score by John Barry and the epic 'feel' of several of the battle and action sequences. Selleck looks the part in his period attire, and he and Armstrong aim for a sort of love-hate chemistry in their exchanges. There's a bit of shrillness on her part and a degree of whininess on his, but generally their characterisations work within the context of the story.

With an approximate $15 million budget and a return in the region of $29 million, *High Road to China* was nowhere near the level of an Indiana Jones box-office behemoth, but at least it made money. Those who doubted Selleck's movie star credentials, those implying that his forté lay in television, weren't completely silenced… but they were, for the time being, muted.

Lassiter (1984)

Selleck was heavily involved in getting his next movie off the ground. He personally optioned David Taylor's *Lassiter* script just before starting work on *High Road to China*. The term "optioning" means that someone (in this case,

Tozer (Bess Armstrong), who needs a flier to help her get to the Himalayan regions of Afghanistan and China, where she hopes to find her father Bradley (Wilford Brimley). She has just twelve days to locate him and confirm he is still alive; otherwise, his business partner will assume total ownership of the family finances. When they eventually find him, Bradley is busily helping the local militia in a small Chinese kingdom defend themselves against a marauding warlord, and Eve and O'Malley get caught up in the fighting.

It's a decent role for Selleck as the grouchy, haunted pilot who has lost his way in life and finds solace at the bottom of a bottle. While Eve initially irritates him, he belatedly realises she, and the mission she has recruited him for, give him renewed purpose. He's quite a flawed hero, often unlikable, sometimes seeking the cowardly way out. But when the chips are truly down, his heroic colours shine through.

The plot is a little rambling and some of the adventures they encounter along the way seem random, not really connected to the bigger quest. They're almost like unrelated mini-episodes, such as the sequence involving Brian Blessed as a fearsome warlord. There's also an annoying subplot featuring Robert Morley as Brimley's business partner. He spends the movie being updated about Eve's progress as she searches for her father, but for some unfathomable reason these scenes are played for comedy, with Morley babbling his frustration while his nervous messenger mugs

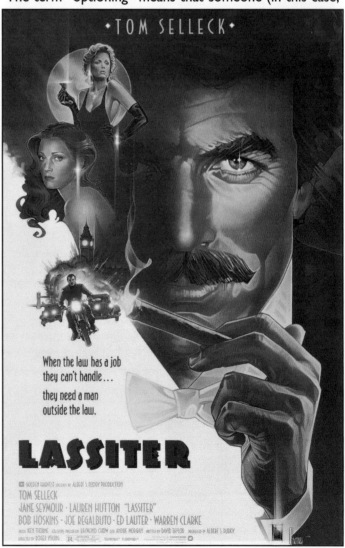

Selleck) secures the exclusive right to buy the screenplay at a later date after successfully pitching the concept to a production company and securing financing. Selleck approached Albert S. Ruddy of Golden Harvest - the production company responsible for *High Road to China* - midway through shooting, and arranged a meeting to pitch his ideas for *Lassiter*. "I thought it was good to have another film lined up in case *High Road* didn't work out," he explained later. Ruddy liked the proposal and the wheels were soon in motion.

The plot revolves around an American cat burglar living in London in 1939. Nick Lassiter (Selleck) makes a living scaling buildings, picking locks, busting safes and vanishing into the night. His eventual goal is to make enough to retire to exotic climes with his girlfriend Sara (Jane Seymour). His plans are jeopardised when the FBI and the British police force, represented respectively by G-man Breeze (Joe Regalbuto) and tough-as-nails copper Becker (Bob Hoskins), apprehend Lassiter and threaten to fake evidence which will land him a twenty-year stretch in jail. He has a choice, though. They will drop all charges and leave him alone if he will do a job for them. The job involves infiltrating the German embassy in London and stealing a fortune in jewels (which are going to be used to fund Nazi Germany's impending war effort). The gems are under the personal protection of Kari Von Fursten (Lauren Hutton), an aristocrat with sadomasochistic tendencies and a penchant for murder.

When it became clear *High Road to China* was going to make a modest profit for Golden Harvest, Selleck began to have second thoughts about *Lassiter*. He realised two period action films in a row might not be a good idea as it could result in typecasting. But, as had been the case with the Indiana Jones role, his strong sense of moral responsibility prevailed, and he agreed to honour his commitment by starring in the film.

The result is fairly mixed. Although set in 1939, *Lassiter* has little feel for the era and never truly convinces as a "period piece". The plot and characters are generally quite cliched - a dashing hero with criminal tendencies, a put-upon girlfriend who worries every time her man goes to work, a ruthless cop determined to screw up the hero's life, a thuggish bodyguard, an ever-reliable sidekick who comes to the hero's aid from time to time... they're all here and they all act and speak exactly as you'd expect. It's like they've been lifted from a 'Stock Character list' that every period action-drama ought to include.

Having said that, the film looks handsome (no surprise there, with Gil Taylor of *The Omen* and *Star Wars* on cinematographic duties) and is consistently slick and watchable within its predictable parameters. The actors do solid work despite the mostly two-dimensional material. Selleck particularly enjoyed the chance to be pro-active, having more input in script alterations and directorial decisions than would usually be the case. Alas, *Lassiter*'s initial theatrical gross was $17.5 million, somewhat down on its $20 million budget. It would need home video and television revenue to eventually recoup its costs, meaning that from a commercial point of view it was a flop. The jury was still out on Selleck's credentials as a big-screen star.

Runaway (1984)

Michael Crichton was masterful at concocting 'near-future' stories. Not novels or movies set decades or even centuries in imaginary futures, but rather ones which were set in a time period just a few years ahead of the point they were written. His works in the genre included the likes of *Westworld*, *The Terminal Man* and *Looker*, and he would go on to write the mammoth bestseller 'Jurassic Park' and its sequel 'The Lost World' (both filmed by Steven Spielberg).

Selleck had a bit-part in the Crichton-directed medical thriller *Coma* in 1978, and they reunited for *Runaway* in 1984. It was the actor's first stab at sci-fi and its futuristic backdrop provided a marked contrast to the two period films he had just made.

He plays a cop named Jack Ramsay who works for the 'runaway department'. As envisaged by Crichton, robots and electronic devices have become commonplace in this futuristic setting, but from time to time they malfunction and trained specialists are called upon to bring the resulting mayhem under control. Ramsay began working for the 'runaway department' after failing to protect his wife from a killer due to his fear of heights. Other than the occasional electric shock, he considers it a safe, predictable and fairly routine line of work. He tells his new partner Karen (Cynthia Rhodes) not to expect much excitement. Most of their callouts can be resolved by flipping a switch.

All that changes when robots suddenly start killing people. It takes a while for Ramsay to realise the robots involved have had their circuitry tampered with. He discovers that a maniacal genius, Charles Luther (Gene Simmons), has developed a chip which overrides a robot's safety features and causes it to attack specific human targets. Luther plans to sell the chips on the black market and Ramsay must stop him. Among Luther's other ingenious inventions are smart bombs, acid-injecting spiderbots and a heat-seeking bullet which can zero in on a chosen target by swerving around corners whilst in flight.

Some aspects of *Runaway* are surprisingly prescient, demonstrating Crichton's ability to anticipate scientific progress and innovations. Also, by giving us a hero with a chronic fear of heights, he sets the stage for an inevitable vertigo-inducing climax which is suspensefully done. The problem is that the movie settles for being a standard chase thriller for most of the running time and doesn't explore its intriguing ideas as much as we'd like. It's less than the sum of its parts, leaving viewers wishing the ideas were developed just a little more.

Simmons of the rock band KISS looks suitably demented as the villain and has a few good lines. Selleck's hero is a more straightforward type, requiring little of the actor other than to look handsome and behave with compassion, courage and tenacity. It's not a role which flexes his acting muscles, but it does require a mix of charm and toughness which he provides in spades.

"To me, there's no point writing a highly cinematic book or doing a very literary movie," Crichton explained later. That's why *Runaway* is brisk and lively, with a busy, eye-catching visual style. The robot designs are imaginative, and the action sequences have a certain flashy energy. But the critical reaction was mixed, and once again Selleck found himself in a movie which underperformed on a commercial level. He was going from strength to strength on TV thanks to *Magnum P.I.* but transferring those accolades, that success, to the big screen continued to prove elusive.

3 Men and a Baby (1987)

After *Runaway*, Selleck continued to make his hit TV show *Magnum P.I.* (the character even appeared in an episode of *Murder, She Wrote*) but his big-screen career stalled for a few years. His comeback occurred in the comedy genre, playing one of three ill-prepared bachelors who end up looking after a baby girl when she is abandoned on their doorstep. The story had been filmed before as *Trois Hommes et un Couffin* (1985) starring Michel Boujenah, André Dusollier and Roland Giraud. It was common in Hollywood for successful French comedies to be remade in English, and this was to prove one of the most commercially successful examples of that practice ever.

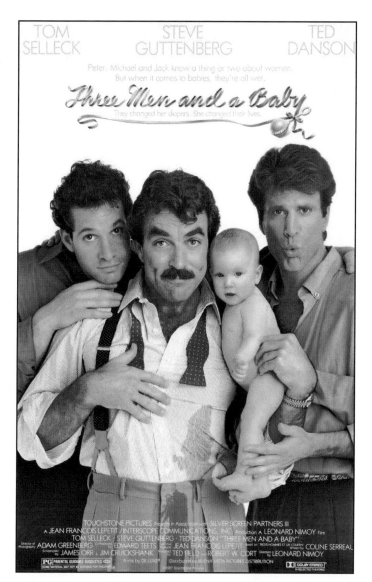

Architect Peter Mitchell (Selleck), satirist Michael Kellam (Steve Guttenberg) and struggling actor Jack Holden (Ted Danson) share a New York apartment and live a carefree bachelor lifestyle. Things change when a baby girl is abandoned on their doorstep with a note from the missing mother explaining that Jack, unbeknownst, is the infant's father. Unfortunately, Jack is away with work at the time, so Peter and Michael end up having to care for the baby despite not having a clue what to do.

Over time, they learn to be good parents and grow attached to the child. Jack returns from his overseas acting gig and, after initially finding his parental responsibilities overwhelming, comes to love the child. A subplot is thrown in involving the three guys being mistakenly suspected of heroin smuggling, and they must draw upon their combined ingenuity to clear their names while raising the baby.

Directed by Leonard (*Star Trek*) Nimoy, *3 Men and a Baby* proved a monster success in 1987, topping the North American box office chart at year's end with a staggering $168 million gross. When worldwide takings were added, that figure was closer to $240 million. Disney had released it under their Touchstone Pictures banner and it became the most successful live-action picture they had released to that point.

Top-billed, Selleck proves himself a slick and easy-going light comedian and revels in poking fun at his macho persona. Guttenberg and Danson, both more readily associated with comic roles, look relaxed and totally at home with the material. Selleck seems a riskier choice because he's out of his comfort zone, but he handles the mix of schmaltz, drama and farce with real aplomb. So much so that for the next decade or so he would land frequent comedy roles in flicks like *Her Alibi* (1989), *3 Men and a Little Lady* (1990), *Folks!* (1992), *Mr. Baseball* (1992), *In & Out* (1997), *The Love Letter* (1999) and the smash TV comedy *Friends* (1994-2004).

While some might consider *3 Men and a Baby* excessively populist and utterly 'safe' Hollywood fare, it cannot be denied that it was a massive hit. After three big-screen starring roles which had been solid and competent but hadn't generated significant financial success, Selleck had finally hit paydirt. For the first time in his career, he was part of a cinematic release which exceeded the enormous popularity of his television work. The nagging suspicion that he might only be able to cut it on the small screen was wiped out for good.

Her Alibi (1989)

Selleck's next feature, another comedy, was his most inconsequential and lightweight of the decade. It was also his first film after *Magnum P.I.* had come to an end. *Her Alibi* casts him as Philip Blackwood, a once-prolific author of mystery novels who is going through a period of

Falling for a beautiful woman can be murder!

TOM SELLECK is
Her Alibi
A Romantic Comedy

WARNER BROS. PRESENTS
A KEITH BARISH PRODUCTION
TOM SELLECK
HER ALIBI
PAULINA PORIZKOVA
WILLIAM DANIELS
JAMES FARENTINO
EDITED ANNE GOURSAUD, A.C.E.
PRODUCTION DESIGNER HENRY BUMSTEAD
DIRECTOR OF PHOTOGRAPHY FREDDIE FRANCIS
MUSIC GEORGES DELERUE
EXECUTIVE PRODUCER MARTIN ELFAND
WRITTEN CHARLIE PETERS
PRODUCED KEITH BARISH
DIRECTED BRUCE BERESFORD

prolonged writer's block. Try as he might, he cannot come up with inspiration for a new novel.

He starts hanging around in courtrooms hoping to strike upon ideas, and one falls into his lap when he sees a young Romanian woman, Nina (Paulina Porizkova), brought in on a charge of murder. Without much evidence to support the notion, Philip decides the girl can't possibly be guilty and offers to provide her with a false alibi. He arranges for her to be released into his custody and takes her to his mansion, hoping her presence will get his creative writing juices flowing. Soon, he begins to wonder if he is harbouring a real murderer - she seems uncannily handy with knives, frequently injures Philip, and wears creepy face paint at night. Has he put himself in a perilous situation, or is there another explanation?

There are some funny scenes and Selleck's witty voiceover provides many of the best moments. He narrates the story the way it is written in his book, exaggerating his own smoothness, heroism and ingenuity. The on-screen action, by contrast, shows him to be accident-prone, cowardly and inept. Ultimately, the story is very slight, and the eventual explanation for Nina's behaviour is quite obvious from early on, meaning there's little surprise when the denouement is reached.

Interestingly, Selleck and Porizkova's relationship on set deteriorated so badly that they weren't speaking by the end of the shoot. It's not clear what their beef was about, but the 20-year age gap might have been a factor. The theatrical poster - showing Porizkova wearing a man's tweed jacket, half concealing a knife, while Selleck stands behind with his arms wrapped around her - wasn't

photographed with the two actors in the same space. Two separate photos were taken and superimposed later to make it look like the actors were together, embracing, when in fact they were not!

Her Alibi is light, breezy and harmless. It didn't make much money (nor did it lose any) and isn't particularly remembered nowadays, but it passes an hour and a half tolerably enough.

An Innocent Man (1989)

For his last movie of the '80s, Selleck, recognising he was in danger of fast becoming a comedy star, moved outside his comfort zone by starring in *An Innocent Man*, a tough, gritty, foul-mouthed prison drama by the versatile English director Peter Yates (of *Bullitt*, *The Deep* and *Krull*). Selleck's character, Jimmy Rainwood, starts out very much like the kind of character you'd expect him to play - an aircraft engineer, thoroughly decent, who dotes on his wife Kate (Laila Robins). For the first thirty minutes, it's a case of Tom Selleck playing Tom Selleck. But all this is just a preamble to something darker than we'd seen him in before.

Two dirty cops, Parnell (David Rasche) and Scalise (Richard Young), are making money by keeping narcotics from drug busts and selling them. They break into Rainwood's house after writing down the wrong address of a drug bust tip-off, and end up shooting Jimmy when they think he is coming at them with a gun (he is, in fact, holding a hair-dryer). To cover their error, they plant evidence at the scene and Rainwood finds himself sentenced to several years of hard time on a totally fabricated drug charge.

During the extended prison sequence in the middle of the movie, we see a new, harder side to Selleck as an actor. Befriended by inmate Virgil Caine (F. Murray Abraham), he is taught the art of survival in the dog-eat-dog world of the penitentiary. He witnesses terrible atrocities within the prison walls and is himself both a victim and perpetrator of extreme violence. He comes out a profoundly changed man, desperate to nail the corrupt cops who put him there in the first place.

An Innocent Man contains some of the expected prison drama cliches but also manages a few fresh angles, especially in its depiction of the unspoken code among inmates. What really sells it is Selleck - he provides the focal point of the story and is the character most of us relate to at the beginning. As we follow him through his dreadful ordeal, we find ourselves imagining how we would handle the same situation, the same horrors, the same pain, the same challenges. Therein lies the strength of the film - the way it gives us an everyman character and puts him (and us) through an intense, frightening and plausible experience. Our emotions are torn by the climax; on one hand, we cheer Rainwood on as he goes after the cops who destroyed his life, but on the other, we feel regret at seeing this once-decent man possessing a newfound taste for violence and a ruthless streak.

Only modestly successful at the box office, *An Innocent Man* shows a completely new, hitherto unseen aspect of Selleck's acting range. For that reason alone, it's worth a look. The icing on the cake is that it's also a good, solid drama with a compelling storyline.

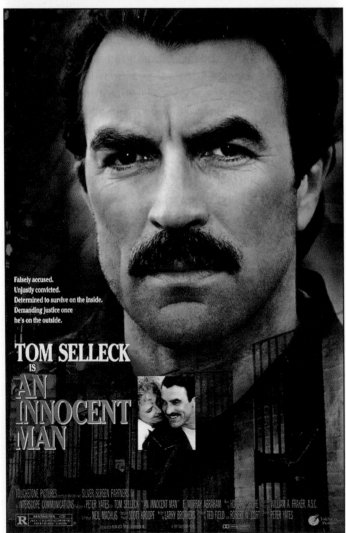

WARREN BEATTY'S MASTERPIECE
REDS

by John H. Foote

Meeting Warren Beatty for an interview a few years ago, I was at once struck by his eyes: alive, curious, intelligent. In fact, they *burned* with intelligence, and during the interview I became aware I was in the presence of a truly brilliant man. He is a major movie star, and though we might not see him on our screens as often as we'd like, he has remained Hollywood royalty for more than fifty years. An artist who walks the line between gifted actor and full-blown movie star, he is often unfairly forgotten despite the array of superb performances he has given down the years.

Take Clyde Barrow in *Bonnie and Clyde* (1967), for example, a film he produced when actors did not do such things. Or his strange cowboy McCabe in Robert Altman's *McCabe and Mrs. Miller* (1971). Or George, the stud hairdresser, in *Shampoo* (1975). Or one of the bungling kidnappers in *The Fortune* (1975). Or his wandering spirit Joe Pendleton in the brilliant *Heaven Can Wait* (1978). Or history-chasing John Reed in *Reds* (1981). Or the comic strip crimefighter *Dick Tracy* (1990). Or the vicious Bugsy Seigel in the crime epic *Bugsy* (1991). Or his bravest, most remarkable performance as a truth-telling, rap-singing politician in *Bulworth* (1998).

Beatty began directing films in 1978 when he co-directed *Heaven Can Wait*. But make no mistake, *he* was calling the shots on that one far more than the co-director Buck Henry. Beatty would later assume solo directing duties for *Reds*, *Dick Tracy* and *Bulworth*, each time challenging himself and pushing himself further as an artist.

It was while visiting Russia in the '60s that he became fascinated with writer John Reed after visiting his tomb (Reed is the only American buried in the Kremlin). Reed's 'Ten Days That Shook the World', an eyewitness account of the Bolshevik Revolution as it happened in 1917, is still widely considered one of the greatest journalistic books ever written. Clean, concise and honest, it is a totally accurate account of what he witnessed. After becoming obsessed with the writer, Beatty felt compelled to make a movie about him. But first he knew he needed to understand more about directing, and to that end he

shadowed Arthur Penn on *Bonnie and Clyde*, observed Altman on *McCabe and Mrs. Miller* and paid close attention to Hal Ashby on *Shampoo* (though it was also said he bullied Ashby while making that film). Ashby later stated: "Warren should have directed the damn thing himself... he is ready!" And ready he was... which he proved beyond doubt when he finally fulfilled his long-held ambition of bringing *Reds* to the screen.

Flash forward to December, 1981. Opening night for *Reds*.

Watching Beatty's massive epic for the first time on the big screen at the beautiful University Theatre in downtown Toronto, I remember being awed. The entire film seemed so intelligent, so perfectly written. Beatty, as director, had captured all the intimate moments

between so many characters, best of all John Reed and Louise Bryant (Diane Keaton). Both were radical writers who travelled to Russia as the Bolshevik Revolution took place and reported about it daily. Reed wrote it all down, and his masterful eyewitness account 'Ten Days That Shook the Word' became perhaps the greatest piece of journalistic writing in existence (at least until Woodward and Bernstein wrote 'All the President's Men').

Beatty had been interested in becoming a director as far back as 1967 when he produced *Bonnie and Clyde*, one of the first major films to usher in the New American Cinema that would develop and explode in the '70s. He was content to learn on *Bonnie and Clyde* by closely watching Penn, the way he was a master of the craft. As noted above, Beatty spent his time on his next few films heeding the work of the directors until, finally, he deemed himself ready to helm a movie of his own. His first effort was the lovely comedy *Heaven Can Wait*, based on the classic '40s film *Here Comes Mr. Jordan* (1941). To help him manage his duties either side of the camera, he hired comic Buck Henry to co-direct with him, but it was mainly Beatty who was in charge. *Heaven Can Wait* was a massive critical and box-office hit, picking up nine Academy Award nominations including four personally for Beatty (Best Picture, Director, Actor and Screenplay), making him the first artist to achieve that distinction since Orson Welles with *Citizen Kane* (1941). Convinced he was now ready to realise his dream project about John Reed, he persuaded Paramount to fund the enterprise to the tune of $32 million. And so began the long process of making *Reds*.

Seeing the finished film in that grand old cinema that December evening in 1981, I was left breathless by what Beatty had achieved. The film was truly astonishing. He had created an intimate epic that was also a grand love story, serving up scenes worthy of David Lean, including a startling ten minutes of the Revolution itself just before the intermission. Filled with intelligence, the actor had waited until he was ready to make an ambitious, important film. His execution, his overall direction, ranks among the great filmmaking achievements in history.

Long before he even started working on it, he travelled across the country to talk to "The Witnesses" - contemporaries of John Reed and Louise Bryant, all now elderly, who'd known them well. These included former friends and enemies who speak to the camera in front of a solid black background. We hear only their remembrances, not the questions that have been put to them, and they are a delight. Henry Miller is as frank and shocking as ever, and the rest are equally wonderful.

The first image we see of Reed defines who he is for the duration of the film. We meet him in Mexico chasing the revolution from the front line alongside Pancho Villa's army. We realise at once that Reed is the kind of man who will forever be chasing history. His writing was always very urgent, giving readers a sense of being in the middle of the very events he was witnessing. It's no surprise that his brilliant reporting in 'Ten Days That Shook the World' is still studied to this day. What interested Reed was the politics of a country - specifically, how that country took care of its people, and what promises were made, then kept or broken, by the government. He came from a wealthy background and understood what wealth was,

what it meant and the power it could bring, yet he did not really care for it and chose to earn his own way through his writing.

In Greenwich Village, he became part of a group of radical scribes who wrote about the American work force and became their voice against their oppressors. Among his friends were the anarchist Emma Goldman (played in *Reds* by Maureen Stapleton) and the great poet and playwright Eugene O'Neill (Jack Nicholson in the film). Collectively, they spoke and wrote with great urgency about what was transpiring in the world at that period. Reed married Louise Bryant, a forward-thinking woman who, under his spell, became a great writer for women's rights and was alongside him to witness the Bolshevik Revolution in 1917. She also helped him edit his masterpiece. Their marriage was often contentious, and her affair with O'Neill was well documented, as was the poet's devastation when she spurned him for Reed. The key factor in her choosing Reed was that they *inspired* one another, brought out the best in each other, both as human beings and as artists (the latter in particular). Bryant was stunned, for example, that in Russia women had the right to vote (they didn't have that right in America at the time), and with Reed's encouragement she was driven to become a tireless advocate of women's rights.

They returned to America to speak and write about what they experienced in Russia. Soon after, Reed was

asked to return and, to her dismay, he did. When he left, she made it clear she might not be there for him when he came back. In the film, she hears nothing from him for months and eventually learns he has been imprisoned in Finland while trying to cross the border. She smuggles herself into the country, crossing a *Zhivago*-like wilderness to the Russo-Finnish border. But she arrives too late and discovers he has been moved back to Russia as part of a prisoner exchange arrangement. She makes her way to Petrograd and discovers he has been sent to Baku in the Middle East to deliver a speech. She hopes to greet him upon his return. He arrives in Petrograd aboard a smashed train, riddled with bullets. Bodies are brought out covered on stretchers, and she begins to fear the worst when there is no sign of him disembarking. Then, in a brilliantly directed moment, we see him behind her before she sees him. The scene is masterly, building to that famous embrace used on the theatrical posters. Reed says to her: "please don't leave me" but it is to be a short-lived reunion as he dies from typhus a short while later with Louise at his side in the hospital.

Visionary? Yes! Stunning? Absolutely. Where does one start when showering praise upon *Reds*?

As a director, Beatty proved himself extraordinary, with

a clear vision of what he wanted. He fills the screen with epic scenes, like the Revolution itself, or a montage which plays over the final minutes of the first act to the strains of the The Internationale. The common folk take Russia; Lenin at last takes to the podium as leader; the scene cuts back and forth through the beautifully lit streets as the Bolsheviks march, taking over the city, while Reed and Louise in the midst of the danger see and understand each other clearly for the first time. Beatty portrays them as observers to the history unfolding in front of them. In many ways, the film matches the intimacy and the beauty and the epic sweep of *Dr. Zhivago* (1965) or even *Gone with the Wind* (1939). Another magnificently directed sequence shows Reed aboard a train travelling to Baku. Again, a Russian theme plays on the soundtrack and Reed opens the curtain of his window to see camels prancing through the stunning vista of the desert. Upon arriving at his destination, he finds a scarecrow of Uncle Sam being burned, which serves only to make him homesick and very aware of the freedom he has given up and the sad fact that he is being used by the Bolsheviks.

Yet for all the astounding epic moments in *Reds*, the small, intimate moments are what make it the work of art it is.

The performances are exquisite. An extraordinary ensemble of actors bring the history to vivid life. Beatty is superb as Reed, an intellectual who understands the theories of communism (without himself being a communist). He knows being with Louise makes them both better writers; similarly, he knows she has cheated on him with his best friend O'Neill. We are left questioning whether Reed, for all his intellect, truly understands love. Does anyone? The passion Reed had for his work, his writing, his pursuit of history as it was unfolding in real time, was akin to the love and devotion Beatty had for his film. Beatty refused to yield to anyone in making the picture exactly as he wanted, prioritising it over friendships and over life itself, becoming obsessed with it. If Reed's writing was the great love of his life, then bringing *Reds* to the screen was Warren Beatty's great passion.

As Bryant, Keaton gives one of the finest performances of her career. An early feminist who continues to expand as a person and to grow as a human being thanks to Reed, she recognizes how the people surrounding her help make her a better writer too. Eugene O'Neill, Emma Goldman, Max Eastman… all of them urge her to write about what is happening in the world. Reed captures the urgency of it all, and he and Louise become lovers and comrades. Driving her always is a burning ambition to raise the profile of women in general - she knows she is not taken seriously because of her sex, and it enrages her.

Jack Nicholson is quietly astonishing as the playwright Eugene O'Neill, a bitter, caustic man who might have been driven to alcohol by Louise's rejection of him. Their affair damaged him deeply, and though he would encounter her again, indeed often, he always managed to stab her with words, which in his hands were worse than a blade of any kind. Seething with burning sexuality, Nicholson moves slowly in the film, speaking clearly with great deliberation, choosing every word carefully like weapons. His words sink in, hit their mark, make their point. He wields vocabulary like ammunition, knowing exactly the impact it is going to have. It is a deep, darkly sexual performance, and we feel the heat between him and Louise and understand what each sees in the other. Equally, we understand how Louise ultimately used O'Neill. Nicholson deserved to win an Oscar for this superb supporting performance - it remains among his greatest screen achievements.

Veteran actress Maureen Stapleton enjoys the role of her career as anarchist Emma Goldman, deported to Russia for her outspoken beliefs. Direct and brutally honest, she is the first person to make clear she does not think Louise is intelligent enough to keep up with their radicalism, just as she is the first to admit she was wrong about her. A tiny, bundled-up force of nature, Stapleton as Goldman is remarkable. She walks away with every scene she's in, leaving us wanting more. Stapleton makes us understand exactly why America feared Goldman enough to deport her, however unconstitutional doing so might have been.

Shortly before, and after, the release of *Reds*, the reviews from North American critics poured in. They declared it a masterpiece, some calling it the greatest American film since *The Godfather*, or, going back further, *Citizen Kane*. Beatty's direction was singled out in reviews - his brilliance, courage and artistry. His genius.

Reds won the coveted New York Film Critics Award for Best Picture and Beatty was among the runners up for Best Director. On the west coast, the Los Angeles Film Critics deemed the film Best Picture, awarding Beatty as Best Director and Stapleton as Best Supporting Actress. Beatty won the Golden Globe for Best Director, and then earned the Directors Guild of America Award for the same. It was a huge honor for any director, but it was the second year in a row the award went to an actor!

Then came the stunner. *Reds* was nominated for twelve Academy Awards, the most by any film in fifteen years. Beatty was personally nominated in four categories - Best Picture, Actor, Director and Screenplay (as co-nominee). Other nominations included Best Actress (Keaton), Best Supporting Actor (Nicholson), Best Supporting Actress (Stapleton), Best Cinematography, Best Sound, Best Production Design, Best Costume Design and Best Film Editing. Going into to Oscar night, *Reds* was the runaway choice to sweep most of the awards (though it was a foregone conclusion that Henry Fonda would beat Beatty for Best Actor). As the night unfolded, there was a tidal wave of support for *Chariots of Fire* (1981), a very average film about Olympic runners - certainly not a film for the ages, more a film of the moment. *Reds* won Best Cinematography and Best Supporting Actress, and Beatty won his well-deserved Best Director award. But then Keaton lost out as Best Actress to Katherine Hepburn in *On Golden Pond* (1981) and, in a shock moment (that I'm not sure I've ever recovered from) *Chariots of Fire* won Best Picture. *Chariots of Fire*!!! Beatty looked crestfallen, like someone had beaten him up. Rarely have I seen a man who had moments earlier won a Best Director Oscar look so defeated, but he did.

Reds didn't make a lot of money. The over-three-hour length made it a hard sell at cinemas and when it came out on video it wasn't exactly a huge rental hit. Thank God for DVD and later Blu-ray - it now enjoys renewed popularity with audiences who have rediscovered the excellence of Beatty's masterpiece.

Reds is a remarkable film, made with passion and honesty, created with agonizing detail and absolute love. It is an '80s classic.

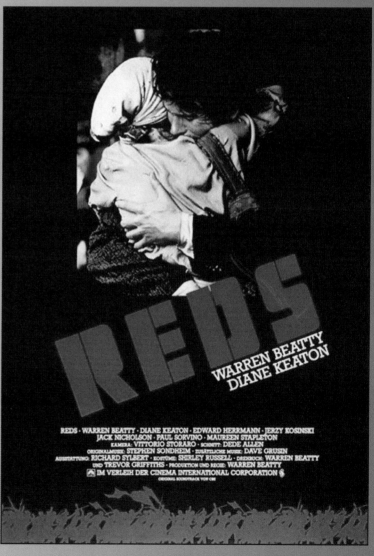

White Dog

by Steven West

"This isn't a Lassie movie. You know what I mean?" - Sam Fuller, Feb 1982.

You find the most disturbing 'monsters' of '80s movies in surprising places. Take Wilber Hull, for example, who appears near the end of Sam Fuller's *White Dog* and is played by veteran character actor Parley Baer. By this stage in his long screen career, Baer had the appearance of an avuncular grandfatherly figure, and here bears a chocolate box gift with a warm grin and the sartorial choices of any typical grandad, while accompanied by two cute granddaughters (one played by Fuller's daughter Samantha). Baer was a familiar face for Americans in particular, notably as the Mayor of Mayberry in *The Andy Griffith Show,* alongside an assortment of sheriffs, generals, scientists and neighbours over the decades. Here, his mask of kindness and sincerity slips suddenly. When confronted, he admits inducting his pet dog into racial violence and we are reminded of the horrors beneath the most disarmingly ordinary faces. Baer was proud of his cameo in the film. Indeed, it summarises *White Dog's raison d'etre* - that often racism, like true evil, presents itself with a smile and a handshake.

Recent news has an alarmingly frequent way of reminding us of people like Wilber. Take Lanarkshire Youtuber Mark Meechan, for example, who trained his partner's pug to respond to Nazi commands on camera, resulting in millions of online views and a public/legal debate about whether his endeavours represented a hate crime or an expression of dark humour. The courts ruled his video anti-Semitic, aggravated by religious prejudice. Joke or not, the dog had been conditioned by Meechan to mimic behaviours from the 20th century's darkest years. Also captured on video soon after, albeit across the Atlantic, was a black man named Jeffrey Ryans being attacked by a dog named Tuco in Salt Lake City. Ryans was on his knees with hands in the air at the time, and the dog was under the orders of the officers at the scene.

When Hitler considered the German Shepherd an essential symbol of the Aryan race, using the dogs to patrol concentration camps, he was neither setting a precedent nor concluding an abhorrent trend. The specifically selected and trained creatures found a vocation as perennial police dogs, infamously being used to attack black protestors in the 1960s American South - images also captured for posterity - and their equivalents in California six decades later, following the fallout of George Floyd's murder. Centuries earlier, the 'war dogs' of Spanish conquistadors pursued and tore apart indigenous people, while Cuban bloodhounds were trained to sense the race of their prey and assault rebel slaves. At a key stage of their development, the dogs used by French generals in early 19th century Haiti were coached to attack a crude wicker figure simulating a black enemy.

Fuller, who stood against fascism in the military, referred to his films collectively as multi-racial, and sought to cast people of colour in complex, empathetic roles at the core of his features, like *The Steel Helmet* (1951), *The Crimson Kimono* (1959) and *Shock Corridor* (1963). Ed Naha of 'Fangoria' was among the journalists who struggled to define *White Dog* (settling on "bizarre melodrama"). It undoubtedly defies easy definition, with Fuller characteristically cutting through the bullshit, describing the need to reach America's prospective racists while they're still young enough to have their prejudices challenged and changed. His character-driven thriller offers a condemnation of the enduring human process of reprogramming canines to service a specific racist agenda. Specifically, he follows the efforts of a sympathetic female protagonist to save one such dog which has been schooled to view black people as an enemy that must be taken down.

Horror cinema's bid to offer the polar opposite of benign, heroic family movie dogs is most famously represented by Lewis Teague's intense Stephen King adaptation *Cujo* (1983), making the fictional St. Bernard's name synonymous with a 'Bad Dog'. In the same period, Greta the Rottweiler in *Satan's Dog* (1982) initiated bathtub-electrocutions and dog-lead strangulations courtesy of its black magic-practising owner Yvonne De Carlo, a low-budget echo of the four-legged agent-of-Satan in *The Omen* (1976). Alan Ormsby's *Dogs of Hell* (1983) also deployed Rottweilers, that most tabloid-demonised of breeds, in a story where they're trained and equipped with surgical implants which transform them into remotely controllable military weapons.

Fuller's serious dramatic take on the theme followed his dismal Hollywood experience with *The Big Red One* (1980), ultimately cut to half its intended length by producers. Needing to move on, he was enticed by the prospect of a return to location shooting for *Let's Get Harry*, but that ended up being helmed by Stuart Rosenberg and released in 1986, with a story credit for Fuller.

As things turned out, Fuller's next directorial outing would prove to be *White Dog*, based on a Romain Gary novel. First published in abridged form by 'Life' magazine in the late '60s, Gary's novel *Chien Blanc/White Dog* was inspired by a lost dog showing up at the home he

shared with his actress-wife Jean Seberg. The story also featured a parallel plot about Seberg's involvement with the Black Panthers. Fuller, who had known the author as a French consul in '50s L.A, disliked what he deemed to be the racist overtones in the plot about the dog's reconditioning (mainly that a black character retrains it to attack whites). Carrying over little more than the core concept of the 'white dog', Fuller crafted a story featuring a black anthropologist named Keys, an actress heroine and a different ending. His loyalty to the project's origins can still be spotted, manifested via an onscreen dedication to Gary and the fact that the lead characters share initials with Gary and Seberg (Roland Gray, Julie Sawyer).

Hollywood had been striving to adapt it for years. Curtis Hanson, enroute to directing the '90s hits *The Hand that Rocks the Cradle* and *L.A. Confidential*, wrote an initial script for Paramount during the Robert Evans era, with post-*Chinatown* Roman Polanski groomed as director. At least half a dozen subsequent drafts were linked to rising filmmakers like Tony Scott and actresses including Jodie Foster. Fuller and Hanson collaborated on the final version and the picture was shot in 43 days for around $7 million. The talented Kristy McNichol, not yet 20 but an Emmy-winner as the tomboy daughter in ABC's popular *Family* (1976-80), was cast as the female lead. The late Paul Winfield, superb as Martin Luther King in NBC's 1978 mini-series *King*, was an astute choice to play Keys.

Fuller was no stranger to allegories, studies of racism and a matter-of-fact approach to contentious subject matter. The genre framework also allowed him to toy with what audience might expect of a conventional killer dog horror film. Fast-cut, carefully angled attack scenes face the usual challenge of turning ostensibly loveable domestic animals into monsters: close-ups of gnashing teeth, bloodied white fur and amplified growls on

the soundtrack. A sequence of the dog crashing through a second-floor window in dramatic slo-mo to pounce upon a human antagonist precedes *Cujo*'s fashionable post-*Carrie* climactic shock.

The dialogue acknowledges literary horror, referring to the white dog as Mr. Hyde (with Keys' mission to find the inner Jekyll) and the most famous fearsome fictional mutt of all, *The Hound of the Baskervilles*. Fuller noted specific reference points, likening the dog's escape from a compound to a Bogart/Cagney jail break, and viewing the story as a modern

Frankenstein, with the strenuous efforts to domesticate the animal echoing the tragic shifts in James Whale's iconic films, like Karloff's creature being forced by persecution and prejudice to abandon the kindness he has learned from others. For Paramount, this added up to a marketing nightmare: the studio's final trailer cut together visceral attack moments while avoiding any trace of the racial angle which was key to the story. If you didn't know better, you'd think it a film about a dog trained to attack... people.

Fuller's final Hollywood film sets its scene via one of Ennio Morricone's most underrated scores. An elegiac main title theme introduces a growing sense of menace to a suitably melancholic melody. We witness only the aftermath of Julie's catalytic accident on a wintry road in the Hollywood Hills. Fuller makes us wait for larger-scale action, including a set-piece of a snowplough crashing through a department store. Julie, a struggling actress currently stuck with a two-line stewardess role, takes home the wounded German Shepherd struck by her car and comes to realise its worth as a guard dog when her home is invaded by an opportunistic criminal.

The intense latter scene, involving what the cops insensitively refer to as "the same damn rapist we nailed last year", confirms a core theme of the endless cycle of violence perpetrated by humans against their own (and other) species. While Julie fends off her assailant with 'final girl'-like resilience, the dog watches explosions and gunfire on TV before savaging the perpetrator. Fuller has fun with movie references elsewhere, casting himself as Julie's agent and cult movie mainstay Paul Bartel as the disgruntled cameraman of her film, bemoaning the

Truffaut-quoting director's artistic use of hokey rear-projected canal footage for her gondola sequence. This initially comic interlude shifts tone when Julie's co-star is attacked, inadvertently announcing the dog's propensity for violence against non-whites.

Fuller's cynicism about the movie business extends to other sectors of L.A. Julie turns to the experts for help and finds the vets keen to monetise her adopted dog while casually predicting a three-day stay at the pound ending in its destruction if it is not claimed. Apparently, the public wants to adopt cute puppies, not their less appealing elders. A harrowing animal shelter sequence depicts dingy, cramped conditions where Julie bears witness to in-house euthanasia. Her unsympathetic boyfriend (Jameson Parker) talks like a horror movie character, spouting trailer-bound one-liners like: "You got a four-legged time bomb!"

The bleakness of mankind's treatment of its 'Best Friend' is balanced with charming light relief. Early scenes at Burl Ives' Noah's Ark - a famous home for animal actors (look out for Dick Miller as a trainer) - offer welcome humour. When not enthusing about a panther who knows every camera angle, Ives shows empathy to the dog's plight and delightfully claims that his own hand helped John Wayne (in *True Grit*'s rattlesnake scene) to win the Oscar. Ives' role also has melancholic undertones - accurately predicting the story's outcome ("Nothing I can do for an attack dog gone bad," he declares) and hurling syringe darts at an R2D2 poster because that "piece of tin" effectively spells the demise of his 40-year business.

Fuller loved the complexity of Winfield's unconventional

'hero' Keys, whose Ahab-like fixation on a non-scientific cure for the white dog doubles as a potential symbolic victory in the war against bigotry. The maverick dog trainer is portrayed by a naturally charismatic actor, with Winfield bringing pathos to the picture's most powerful dog attack: a discreet church-set fatality largely played off a reaction shot of Keys, tears streaming down his face when witnessing another victim of society's sickness. Keys is no saint - he is self-aggrandising and sometimes aloof, and sets a grim deadline (if he can't retrain the dog in five weeks, he'll kill it). He serves as the Quint-style expert often found in eco-horror films, the guy who understands (and can potentially overcome) the natural threat. For the benefit of the naïve Julie (and the audience), Keys offers a potted history of the various white dogs over time, conditioned by violence, fear and hate to keep a horrific tradition alive.

Keys makes significant breakthroughs, but the sickness runs too deep. The final test offers a palm-sweating finale propelled by Morricone's stirring suspense cues, and a near-silent wrap-up with a wrenching reminder that hoped-for victories don't come easy. Such a pessimistic conclusion would have rattled any Hollywood studio, but the subject matter alone made Paramount nervous. Fuller was affronted by a set visit by Willis Edwards of the National Association for the Advancement of Coloured People to determine if his film was presenting an objectionable image of black people. Edwards was ordered off the set and Fuller advised the NAACP to see the movie to decide for themselves. He maintained: "If anyone complains about this movie, it will be the Klan."

The negative publicity nonetheless resulted in Paramount shelving the picture's intended theatrical run and nixing a U.S. video release. The director likened its suppression to a newborn baby being jailed. His faith in Hollywood at a new low, he took refuge in Europe where he made three more features. Later cable showings and screenings in New York and Chicago eventually rebuilt *White Dog*'s reputation, and it found ardent admirers like the Jonathan Rosenbaum of the 'Chicago Reader' who celebrated its intelligence and bravery.

Tragically but inevitably, it remains as relevant as ever. Core themes about how we treat our animals and our fellow man

have resurfaced in both narrative films and real-world events. Kornel Mundruczo's harrowing near-namesake *White God* (2014) takes a child's eye view of the fate of a mixed-breed dog, with its four-legged actors trained by Teresa Anne Miller, daughter of the late Karl Lewis Miller, who was the animal trainer on both *White Dog* and *Cujo*. 'Mauled: When Police Dogs Are Weapons' (2021), a Pulitzer winner for National Reporting, delivered a timely examination of the training of dogs to hunt and control black people over the centuries. And, in 2022, Anais Barbeau-Lavalette's *White Dog* returned to the original novel, focusing on Gary and Seberg's symbolic rehabilitation of the dog in late '60s L.A in the wake of Dr. King's assassination.

GIVE MY REGARDS TO BROAD STREET

by Stephen Mosley

In 1964, the Beatles brought a newfound respectability to the rock 'n' roll musical with *A Hard Day's Night*. Its successful blend of 'day-in-the-life' naturalism and surreal humour rejuvenated the teen-oriented genre. Two decades later, Paul McCartney tried to recapture the spirit of his earlier film by writing and starring in *Give My Regards to Broad Street*.

It wasn't the first time that Paul had taken creative control of a film. In 1967, enthused by his own experiments in amateur filmmaking, he commandeered *Magical Mystery Tour*; the main idea of which was to pack the Beatles onto a yellow bus alongside various eccentrics, circus performers and members of the public, and drive around the UK filming whatever happened. As well as providing a script that was little more than a circle divided into sections (one was titled 'Dreams' and, in another, he had simply drawn a smiley face), McCartney also directed many scenes and made key contributions during the editing process.

Magical Mystery Tour was screened on BBC1, in black-and-white, as a Boxing Day treat. Even though it featured such classic, then-new songs as *The Fool on the Hill* and *I Am the Walrus*, the public were not amused by its psychedelic antics. "There was no theme or storyline," one contemporary viewer complained to the BBC, "the programme appearing to consist of confused, disconnected shots of the weirdest things and suggesting a nightmare rather than a mystery tour." A rare disparate view arrived in a letter to the 'Daily Telegraph' from a Mrs. Anne-Lee Michelle of Somerset, dated 30th December, 1967: "We are an elderly couple and have never seen or heard of the Beatles. The film entranced us… I thought it a clever blend of all-too real life and pure magic… The photography was imaginative and original, and I laughed till I cried several times. But I fear they will not make another film like it - and perhaps they had better not try."

These days, most people have come round to Mrs. Michelle's way of thinking: *Magical Mystery Tour* enjoys cult status and is publicly admired by filmmakers as diverse as Martin Scorsese and Terry Gilliam. Paul's 1984 film *Give My Regards to Broad Street,* on the other hand, was similarly lambasted on its release but today's movie-going public have not warmed to it in the same way. The time is ripe for reappraisal.

Despite the perceived failure of *Magical Mystery Tour,* McCartney's interest in film never waned. Aside from starring in the Beatles' fun-filled vehicles, he had composed a strong score for the 1966 film *The Family Way* and was responsible for arguably the best James Bond theme with *Live and Let Die* (1973). By the early '80s, however, providing music for films was no longer enough - he desired to *make* another movie of his own.

Inspired by a real-life incident involving the Sex Pistols, McCartney dreamed up a simple plot: the tapes for his latest album have been stolen and he must get them back. The former Beatle wrote the screenplay in the back of his car during the two-hour drive to and from the studio whilst recording his *Pipes of Peace* album. When shooting began in November 1982, Peter Webb was chosen to direct. Webb's previous experience included an episode of *The Sooty Show*. After *Broad Street*, he never directed again.

Paul's script combined a day-in-the-life view of a working musician with some spirited interpolations of fantasy - a car that whizzes down country roads at abnormal speed,

leaving Sunday drivers flustered in its wake, and a wintry dream sequence set to *Eleanor Rigby*, the imagery of which calls to mind a mix of Charles Dickens and Lewis Carroll. This latter sequence, although impressive in parts, goes on way too long and is a good example of the kind of indulgence for which critics initially panned the film. A typical example came from the 'Daily Mail' who intoned: "Don't see it. Send a wreath and condolences to all concerned."

Give My Regards to Broad Street is not wholly deserving of such a damning verdict. Yes, the storyline lacks dramatic bite - Paul knows who's taken the missing tapes all along and doesn't seem all that bothered about it, anyway. There's some vague threat posed by an icy executive personified by John Bennett in a pair of wraparound shades, but McCartney's unruffled response is to produce unflattering caricatures of the man during board meetings. In fact, Macca coasts through the entire movie in laid-back, nonplussed mode, only coming to life during the musical numbers. But, happily, there are plenty of them.

Opposed to the phoniness of lip-synching, Paul insisted on live performances throughout, which certainly brings an extra charge to the career-spanning song score. During an acoustic medley of *Yesterday* and *Here, There & Everywhere*, he is even reunited with two old friends: George Martin produces at the mixing desk whilst Ringo Starr searches frantically for the right brushes for his drums. Ringo's tomfoolery is not merely for comic effect - the drummer wanted no part in re-recordings of Beatles evergreens, even though Macca's recreations are strong and faithful. Another musical highlight is a performance of *Silly Love Songs* with the band (including wife Linda) made up as bizarre, white-faced aliens.

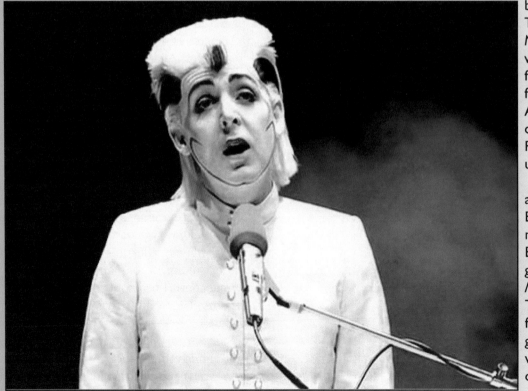

There's also *No More Lonely Nights* - a smashing ballad written especially for the film, which was nominated for both a Golden Globe Award and a BAFTA (it lost out in the latter category to Ray Parker Jr's *Ghostbusters* - understandably).

The cast is also proficient, albeit not given enough to do. Bryan Brown stars as Paul's manager, Ringo's wife Barbara Bach (a memorable Bond girl in *The Spy Who Loved Me*) plays a journalist, and Tracey Ullman, making her film debut, is the sympathetic girlfriend of the scoundrel who nicked the tapes. In one of his final roles, Ralph

Richardson puts in a cameo appearance as Paul's elderly father - an echo of the grandfather character played by Wilfrid Brambell in *A Hard Day's Night*.

Indeed, *Give My Regards to Broad Street* feels to me like a semi-unofficial follow-up to *A Hard Day's Night*, showing us what Paul and Ringo are up to twenty years on. Both musicians continue to project a likeable presence onscreen, their personas charming and insouciant amid the chaos spinning round them. The quirky spirit of *A Hard Day's Night* is also present in such dialogue exchanges as:

A: "There's going to be all kinds of complications that we haven't even thought about yet?"

B: "Yeah? What?"

A: "I haven't thought about 'em yet."

The humour extends into the visuals. During a tea break, the brass musicians all raise their cups in unison as if they are still playing their instruments and later, in another dream sequence, Paul is secretly filmed busking outside Leicester Square tube station. Surprisingly, no one recognised him and he was even tossed a few pennies. Elsewhere, British wrestler Giant Haystacks, of whom McCartney was an unlikely friend and fan, appears as a shady bootlegger with a nice line in fancy coats.

This carefree, anything-goes approach pervades much of *Give My Regards to Broad Street*, bringing to mind such zany

late '60s features as *Casino Royale* and *The Magic Christian* (also starring Ringo, and for which Paul had written the great theme song *Come and Get It*). The trouble is that what seemed to swing in the '60s only amounted to tedium in the doleful grey haze of Thatcher's Britain.

Filming was complete by July 1983, but the movie's release was held back until autumn 1984 so that the ever-busy McCartney could promote *Pipes of Peace*. On its initial cinema screenings, the film was supported by *Rupert and the Frog Song*, a thirteen-minute animation which Paul had written, produced and lent his voice to. This amiable short is best remembered for its hit single, *We All Stand Together* (aka *The Frog Song*).

Along with a best-selling soundtrack album and tie-in book, there was also a *Give My Regards to Broad Street* computer game, in which the player drove around a depressing stretch of road, doing nothing in particular to the infuriating blare of *Band on the Run*. But even this could not prevent the movie from flopping at the box office. Seen today, with its appealing mix of fantasy and music, *Give My Regards to Broad Street* is undemanding entertainment and a perfect escape from the rain.

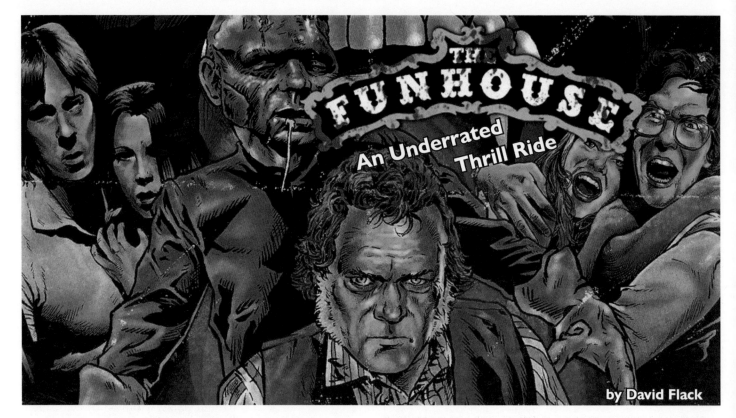

THE FUNHOUSE

An Underrated Thrill Ride

by David Flack

Whenever director Tobe Hooper is mentioned, you can be pretty sure *The Texas Chainsaw Massacre* (1974) will be at the heart of the discussion. Hardly surprising, since it is an important milestone in the history of horror films. Considering its low budget and the problems encountered while making it, it remains an impressive achievement in many ways. I certainly respect its cultural impact but I've always been slightly disappointed with it, finding it rather overhyped. In the UK, it wrongly earned a reputation as some sort of gory bloodbath, which it isn't. The reality is that there is surprisingly little blood in it (not that that is a bad thing). Anyway, I'm not here to discuss the plus and minus points of *The Texas Chainsaw Massacre*. What I'm trying to say is that Hooper came out of it with quite a reputation, and he followed it with a number of other impressive films, the best of which - for me - is his excellent adaption of Stephen King's *Salem's Lot* (1979). My second favourite Hooper film is *The Funhouse* (1981), a little gem that I first saw at the cinema when it was double billed with *My Bloody Valentine* in 1981. I saw it twice more on double bills, and each time I came away impressed by it.

Briefly, the plot follows four teenagers who visit a local carnival and, on a whim, decide to stay overnight in the funhouse. Their night of amusement soon becomes a night of terror after they witness a murder and are stalked by a carnival barker and his hideous freak of a son.

In the late '60s or early '70s, when I was a child of eight or nine years of age, I remember going to fun-fairs in my hometown of Cambridge, England. In those days, fairs were big events offering many attractions like 'The Wall of Death' (motorcycle riding stunts), wrestling and boxing booths, strip shows and freak shows. I always found the freak shows interesting and scary - seeing the garish art advertising what wonders awaited inside would set my pulse racing. This sort of nervous excitement is something *The Funhouse* puts over very well in its early scenes, where the carnival atmosphere is depicted in all its glory. It's one of the many reasons I love the film as much as I do. Another reason is John Beal's memorable, maniacal score which enhances things immensely, creating a feeling of unease right from the opening credits.

The first scene seems to parody the opening of John Carpenter's *Halloween* (1978), with everything seen through the eyes of a character, and ending with a homage to *Psycho* (1960). This scene, like others, offers pointers to events that will come later in the story, some obvious, some subtle.

Of the four main characters, Amy (Elizabeth Berridge) is the more rounded and given the most background. She is a homely girl, not conventionally beautiful but certainly cute. Her boyfriend Buzz (Cooper Huckabee) seems an ill match for her, brash and cocky, but proves himself later. The two other friends - also a couple - are Richie (Miles Chapin) and Liz (Largo Woodruff). Richie initially seems like a nerd, but he's the one who sets the events in motion by coming up with the idea of spending the night in the funhouse. It's also one of his actions - stealing money from the fortune teller's booth - that partly prompts the terrifying events that take place. His girlfriend Liz is initially the more assured and confident of the two girls, but when things get out of control, she becomes understandably frightened and hysterical. All four young actors play their roles well, despite seeming a little too old to be playing teenagers (a common criticism of films of this type). Berridge is especially good - her character is the one the audience generally find themselves rooting for.

There are four other significant characters, including Amy's horror-loving, prank-laying younger brother Joey (Shawn Carson), one of whose practical jokes starts the film. He unwisely tags along on the carnival trip, unknown to the others. He doesn't have a good time of it and, boy, is he made to pay for his misdemeanours! The words spoken by his sister ("I'm going to get you, Joey. I'm really going to get you and you'll never forget it!") come back to haunt him by the end. At the climax, we find ourselves really fearing for the boy's sanity after such a traumatic experience. A particularly disturbing scene involves him falling into the hands of a carnival worker who contacts his parents. When they come to collect him, there is something about the look on the worker's face, something uncomfortable about his comments, which make you wonder just what he has done to the boy. It is left ambiguous but it's hard not to jump to disturbing conclusions - it's one of many scenes which leave you with an uneasy feeling that hideous and sinister things have taken place. There are a number of good jolt scenes; one in particular, featuring Joey, made me nearly jump out of my seat the first time I saw the film.

The fortune teller Madame Zena (Sylvia Miles) is a classic horror comic portrayal, and Miles has obvious fun pulling out all the stops. Garish and over-the-top, her role is small but important. Apparently, she didn't enjoy her participation (thinking the material beneath her) but she keeps her disdain well hidden during the film. Her sex scene with the creature is funny, though it ends badly for Madame Zena. There's another scene earlier, featuring a magician's act with William Finlay (a stalwart of Brian De Palma films), and that scene plus the freakish sex scene are two moments which add a bit of humour to an otherwise

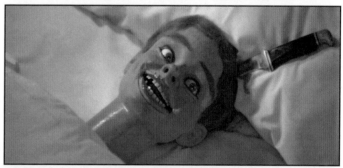

tense and suspenseful film.

The part of the freak show barker is played by Kevin Conway, who appears in three roles in the film (he appears as two other barkers, obviously keeping the carnival business in the family!) He steals every scene he's in, pulling off a complex role very well. He is crafty, ruthless and sleazy with a macabre sense of humour. He also has a certain fragility as demonstrated through his fatherly bond with his freak son. I kept wondering about their relationship, how it came to be the way it is. Hooper drops a hint during a partial conversation in which a carnival worker relates a story to two others. The section of story we catch could well be related to the barker and his freak son, but whether this is so is left tantalisingly and frustratingly open. It gives the film a disturbing feel all the way through.

Then there's the hideous freak son (Wayne Doba), a memorable creature who works for his father as a funhouse helper donned in a boiler suit and a Frankenstein monster mask. The 'monster-from-Frankenstein' reference is entirely deliberate - there is a clear parallel between Mary Shelley's creature and the freak in *The Funhouse*. Both are tragic figures, freaks of nature through no fault of their own. The way Doba moves and his guttural noises and dribbles show that something is not right. He has a vulnerability and innocence and is like a troublesome, difficult-to-handle teenager entering the first stages of puberty. Some of the exchanges with his father, and the sleazy sex scene with madame Zena, show this. You are not given any clues about his exact age, but it seems likely he is quite young. As hideous and repulsive as his appearance is, viewers have a kind of sympathy for him which makes the character more effective.

When his father tells him to find and kill the witnesses, he clearly does not want to do this. There are hints that he has committed other murders in places that the carnival has visited previously. But despite being a vicious killer, we sense his drive to kill is beyond his control. The scene where we first see him in all his repulsive glory is a great scene, indeed for me the highlight of the film. Rick Baker's make up is simple but effective and Doba's mesmerising performance makes the role more than the usual man-in-a-mask monster schtick. His final scene with his father, and the final confrontation with Amy, are very memorable. I knew what the creature looked like before seeing the film because there were plenty of spoilerish publicity photographs doing the rounds at the time. Nonetheless, the big reveal is still a great scene. Doba is a mysterious actor who played parts heavily steeped in make-up and disguises. He had another memorable role as an unfortunate member of a nightclub act hidden in an outsize suit and cartoon head during a machine-gun massacre in Brian De Palma's *Scarface* (1983).

Hooper's direction is assured and he sprinkles the film with references to his earlier, iconic *Texas Chainsaw Massacre* (e.g. the confined location, the two very different families involved, the ending where those who survive are clearly going to have a difficult time recovering from their traumatic ordeal). The film has a little more blood than *The Texas Chainsaw Massacre* but is still less bloody than you might expect. Apparently, Steven Spielberg was suitably impressed with Hooper's work on *The Funhouse*, which is one of the reasons he was entrusted with helming *Poltergeist* (1982). Inexplicably, *The Funhouse* was included for a while on the notorious BBFC Video Nasties list of the '80s (an embarrassing British phenomenon, well worth reading about whichever country you're from). The

list really highlighted the hysterical and totally over-the-top attitude the British media and hypocritical members of parliament had towards horror films at the time. There is nothing in *The Funhouse* which remotely warranted its place on such a list and it was rightly withdrawn fairly early in proceedings. The fact that pretty much all the films named and shamed have since been released in deluxe, uncut versions (some have even appeared on television) proves what a ludicrous episode in hysteria and hypocrisy the whole sorry affair was. I digress, but the more I think about it, the angrier I get! Writers, scholars and film historians better than me have written plenty about it, showing it to be a shameful farce which has been rightly consigned to the realms of distant memory.

Overall, *The Funhouse* is a very good little film and still largely underrated. It often appears on lists of slasher movies, but personally I don't think it should be categorised that way. It's a damn good horror thriller, with many memorable scenes and performances, a frenzied soundtrack and, most of all, a memorable and enduring monster. It has a lot more to offer than standard slasher fare. I can't recommend it highly enough.

The Amateur

by Joe Secrett

Dedicated to Dorothy Golding (1926-2022) - "My late grandma, and my first reviewer."

It's the early '80s and the Cold War becomes considerably hotter during the course of Charles Jarrott's dark and intense spy thriller *The Amateur* (1981). It tells the story of a CIA cryptographer, Charles Heller (John Savage), who is devastated when his beloved fiancée is brutally murdered during a hostage situation in Europe. When the terrorists' demands are subsequently met, they are allowed to escape by plane to Eastern Europe. Heller demands retribution and blackmails the CIA by threatening to leak documents which will incriminate them in past wrongdoings. He wants to be trained and allowed to travel to Czechoslovakia to go after the people responsible for the death of his fiancée. After completing a crash course under the watch of a handler, Anderson (Ed Lauter), he is briefed about his quarry, equipped, and let loose to hunt them down.

The story keeps the audience in an almost constant state of unease. It works primarily as an incredibly realistic approach to modern spy thrillers, indeed spy films in general. It shows the stress of being a field agent in a dangerous environment. Heller is a fish-out-of-water,

with no Bond-style gimmickry or comic-book gadgets and technology to get him out of tight corners. He is given inadequate equipment and crash-course style training before being let loose to carry out a mission he is barely ready for. During his quest for vengeance, he meets frequent hostility from allies and foes alike.

When he arrives in Europe, even his own 'side' seeks to hinder him. The stakes are raised as each day passes, and we end up sympathising with poor Heller as he navigates incredible risks to complete his mission.

Savage downplays his performance for the majority of the running time, though during the tense and shocking opening sequence he's convincingly distraught. Once his mission of vengeance is underway, his attitude becomes darker - brooding, yet still sympathetic. We feel his frustration during his time in the Eastern Bloc; we savor his victories and feel his pain as he strives to avenge his wife to be.

There is minor graphic violence peppered throughout, but nothing is lingered on too much. There are rather clever sequences too, one involving a swimming pool with a glass window looking into a bar, another depicting a brief but bloody shootout in a storehouse. The body count is surprisingly low, but when it comes to people being brutally dispatched there are flashes of gruesomeness. The film opts for quite drab colours to reinforce its bleak undertones and the cynical outlook of its main character. Heller is alone and afraid in a foreign land, not knowing the language; he's a perpetual moving target throughout his ordeal.

The supporting cast features the late, great Christopher Plummer as a senior security service member named Lakos, one of the many people attempting to apprehend Heller. He's only seen a handful of times, but does well with what little he has to work with. His scenes, while brief and infrequent, are pivotal to the story. He's fine as the older agent thrust into the middle of Heller's mission, who gradually comes to respect him because of his tenacity and determination, and becomes a sort of father figure to him towards the finale. It's a nice role for Plummer, and he's always a welcome presence in any movie, be it a mainstream bonanza or one of these more obscure titles.

TV and film veteran Ed Lauter has a fairly active role as Heller's trainer, Anderson. Like Plummer, he gives it his all, and it's good to see him pop up from time to time as the story progresses. He conveys a certain menace, initially reluctant to train Heller but eventually, begrudgingly, accepting of the task. Lauter, a busy actor right up to his death in 2013 (aged 74), appeared in almost every genre imaginable, and had over 200 screen credits to his name, including fairly well-known films such as *The Longest Yard* (1974), the infamous *Death Wish 3* (1985) and the Arnie vehicle *Raw Deal* (1986).

Heading up the villains, as the terrorist leader Schrager, is Nicholas Campbell. Schrager, like Lakos, is not given as much screen time as you'd expect, but he makes his presence known when he's on screen. He has a certain boyish charm in terms of looks and the way he carries himself. Behind

L'HOMME DE PRAGUE
(THE AMATEUR)

© 1982 20th Century Fox tous droits reserves

that are exposed during the running time.

The film is a late entry in the Cold War espionage sub-genre which features the likes of *The Spy Who Came in from the Cold* (1965) and *The Kremlin Letter* (1970). The genre seemed to fall out of fashion soon after following Clint Eastwood's *Firefox* and Jeannot Swarc's *Enigma* (both 1982). It firmly plants its boots in a more down-to-earth setting, nothing like the James Bond and Jason Bourne films in which scores of villains are dispatched with little or no difficulty. The screenplay is by Robert Littel, who worked as a foreign correspondent during the Cold War and whose works often allude to Soviet and CIA activity during that era, which adds to the realism quite well. The story is a little slow in parts, but the performances are excellent and add to the compelling nature of the plot. It's fair to say *The Amateur* runs at a more relaxed pace than most post-2000 films, but personally I think this works in its favour.

Finding the film can be difficult. At the time of writing, DVD copies are quite rare and expensive as it only had a limited release from Anchor Bay many years ago. Currently, no streaming sites seem to carry it in their library either. Who knows, maybe we'll get an upgraded release in the future and finally be able to give this overlooked spy drama the attention it deserves.

Overall, *The Amateur* keeps its twists and turns coming and is a worthwhile and underrated pic. It's not perfect, but it's a very solid thriller which keeps the mystery and intrigue high and boasts exemplary performances all round.

L'HOMME DE PRAGUE
[THE AMATEUR]

In a world of professional assassins, there is no room for an amateur.

At 29, Charles Heller was a mathematician without equal.

At the CIA, he was a computer expert without peer.

But when terrorists murdered the most important woman in his life, he became an assassin without experience.

To avenge her death, the CIA trained him, briefed him, armed him, and then…they abandoned him.

The first 11 minutes will absolutely shock you.

The last 11 minutes will rivet you to your seat.

The Amateur

MARIO KASSAR and ANDREW VAJNA Present A JOEL B. MICHAELS, GARTH H. DRABINSKY Production A CHARLES JARROTT FILM
JOHN SAVAGE
CHRISTOPHER PLUMMER
MARTHE KELLER
"THE AMATEUR" ARTHUR HILL NICHOLAS CAMPBELL GEORGE COE JOHN MARLEY and ED LAUTER Director of Photography JOHN COQUILLON, B.S.C.
Production Designed by TREVOR WILLIAMS Screenplay by ROBERT LITTELL and DIANA MADDOX Based on the Novel "The Amateur" by ROBERT LITTELL
Executive Producers MARIO KASSAR and ANDREW VAJNA Produced by JOEL B. MICHAELS and GARTH H. DRABINSKY
Directed by CHARLES JARROTT Music by KEN WANNBERG
R RESTRICTED

LADYHAWKE

by Darren Linder

Ladyhawke was released in 1985 and is a wonderful, if somewhat flawed, fantasy classic. The main flaw is the music, which can be distracting to the point of completely taking you out of the movie. Luckily the actors, director and, perhaps most importantly, the cinematographer elevate it to such an extent that you can mostly forgive the dated soundtrack missteps. Overall it is a fun combination of adventure, romance and action, guided by a great director.

Someone described this film to me recently as *The Princess Bride* with the silliness and overt comedy removed, and I would have to agree. It takes place in 1386 and deals with numerous castles, animal familiars, crossbow and sword battles, and a nefarious and cruel curse. The film has some serious star power, with Rutger Hauer and Michelle Pfeiffer playing the leads and Matthew Broderick as the character through whose eyes we experience the story (as well as providing a bit of comic relief).

Hauer had recently transitioned to American films after primarily being known for his work in Dutch cinema. *Nighthawks*, *Blade Runner* and *The Osterman Weekend* had all put him on the international map. His screen presence in *Ladyhawke* is undeniable, and he carries the movie. His blond hair and blue eyes captivate the viewer, and he looks damned good atop a black horse with a hawk on his forearm. Pfeiffer had just made a name for herself in films like *Scarface* and *Into the Night*. Her role in *Ladyhawke* is the direct opposite of the unlikeable cokehead moll she played in *Scarface*. Her character Isabeau is every bit as luminous and charming as we would expect her to be.

Matthew Broderick, who had just appeared in *WarGames*, is perfectly cast as Phillipe, the naïve thief of this story. The comments he makes to himself, usually regarding making a deal with God to escape some punishment, are frequently amusing.

The storyline is fairly simple, but expertly told. It skillfully resists revealing the exact details until almost halfway into the film. Navarre and Isabeau, played by Hauer and Pfeiffer, are lovers with a curse put on them by a jealous Bishop. The curse causes Navarre to remain in human form by day, but he transforms into a wolf by night. Isabeau takes human form by night but is a hawk by day. When they are in animal form, they have no memory of the half-life of their human existence. Broderick's character Phillipe sums it up beautifully when the situation is finally explained to him: "Always together, eternally apart." There is the briefest moment at sunrise and sunset when they can almost touch before their transformation. Making things even more difficult is the fact that if the Bishop is killed, the curse will go on forever. But perhaps there is a loophole...

Phillipe: "Are you flesh, or are you spirit?"

Isabeau: "I am sorrow."

Any movie needs a believable and menacing villain, and John Wood's portrayal of the evil Bishop is riveting. He seems interested in his position not for the celebration or the privilege of sharing the Lord's word, but for the personal power it affords him and the pleasure he gleans from instilling fear in others. He embraces pure hypocrisy, preaching the word of love one moment while callously ordering the murder of prisoners and having regular

hangings the next. Like Alan Rickman as the villain Hans Gruber in *Die Hard*, Wood's line delivery absolutely sells it for me. When his Captain of the Guard, Marquet (Ken Hutchison), reports that Phillipe has escaped from the prison of Aquila and that it would have taken a miracle for anyone to have done that, the Bishop replies with palpable weariness and impatience: "I believe in miracles, Marquet… it's part of my job." He snaps at his subordinates and demands they kiss his ring, but he never chews the scenery and never overacts the part. His Bishop embodies the pious, condescending, sanctimonious person-addicted-to-power type that so often gravitate towards the clergy. His aquiline features and piercing glare remind me of the sort of gravity Peter Cushing always brought to his roles. Wood also gets some great lines, like: "Great storms announce themselves with a simple breeze, Captain. And a single random spark can ignite the fires of rebellion."

Another actor in a small role that I loved was Alfred Molina. In this film he plays Cezar, a wolf-hunter hired by the Bishop's Captain to kill Navarre. He may be most recognized as Indiana Jones' untrustworthy companion Satipo from the opening sequence of *Raiders of the Lost Ark* (the guy who is deathly afraid of tarantulas and the Hovitos who he meets his grisly demise after saying the famous line: "You throw me the idol, I throw you the whip.") Molina was also in the climax of *Boogie Nights* as Rahad, the drug dealer who loves listening to mix tapes with *Sister Christian* and *Jessie's Girl* and is buddies with Ricky Springfield. He always impresses, even in small roles such as this one. He certainly has bad luck with dying in movies though. In *Raiders* he gets impaled by spikes, and in *Ladyhawke* he gets his head crushed in a bear trap much like the final scene in Sam Peckinpah's *Straw Dogs* (and, in an amusing connection, Ken Hutchison, who plays Marquet in *Ladyhawke*, also played villain Norman Scutt in *Straw Dogs*).

Ladyhawke is directed by Richard Donner, who helmed such iconic movies as *Superman, The Omen* and all four *Lethal Weapon* entries. He also directed *The Goonies*, which was released a mere two months after *Ladyhawke* in 1985. With such a diverse range of films - including horror, superhero and the buddy cop genre - he added another genre to his catalogue, proving a capable director with this medieval fantasy adventure.

But I believe that the top reason this film is of such quality is the three-time Academy Award-winning cinematographer Vittorio Storaro. This man has been the cinematographer on many great films since the '60s and is still active today at age 82. His filmography is lengthy and impressive, but I particularly love his work because he was the cinematographer on my favorite film of all time, Francis Ford Coppola's Vietnam masterpiece *Apocalypse Now* (1979). He excels at lighting dark dungeons or night shoots. Often when we see Pfeiffer, he casts the entire location in a gorgeous blue hue, since she only takes human form at dusk and then returns to hawk form at sunrise. He filmed these scenes at the crack of dawn to capture that surreal natural lighting that you just can't get by using the day-for-night techniques (shooting in the sunlight and then dimming or darkening the image to convince viewers that it is nighttime). The frame composition of the scenes in the snow, ice or rain is glorious.

Storaro did have the benefit of shooting on location at several castles in Italy. It was fascinating to watch the pulley mechanisms raising huge wooden doors or lowering drawbridges. The vast mountain ranges and landscape shots look beautiful. The first shot of the muck and mud as Broderick's character digs his way out reminded me of the chitinous, dripping residue from the xenomorphs in *Alien*. The inside of the dungeon cells, with stark torch lighting between the wooden slats, is striking. The vast cathedral is lit by hundreds of candles during the climactic mass ceremony that turns into a bloody battle. The actual transformation scenes aren't done with prosthetics or puppets. They chose a more subtle approach of using elaborate editing, lighting changes, shots of shadows of the hawk's wings on Rutger's face, contact lenses that look like animal eyes, etc. They imply the changes rather than attempting to show them. There was no option for any CGI, thank goodness. This film looks far better than it needed to, due to Storaro's skilled eye.

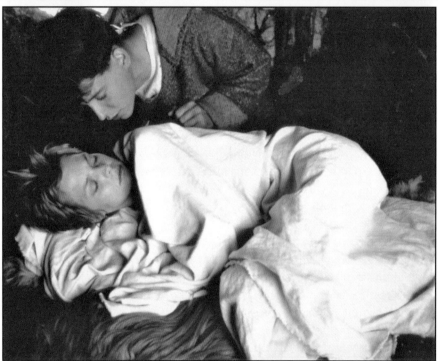

As much as I truly adore this beautiful film, I must make a little time to address the soundtrack problems. Obviously I love films of the '80s, and music choices can make or break a film, either locking you into the fun nostalgia of the time or screaming out with groan-inducing distraction. It sounds like there are two separate musical soundtracks are being utilized in *Ladyhawke*. We either get the overly happy synth tripe that does not fit the movie at all, or we get an actual dramatic score performed by an orchestra. It's hard to determine who is at fault. The credits list Alan Parsons (from the rock group Alan Parsons Project) as producing the music score that is performed by the Philharmonic Orchestra. But Andrew

Powell is also credited with composing and conducting the entire soundtrack. Parsons and Powell were collaborators/partners in the Alan Parsons Project, and both played keyboards, But since the two music styles are so different, I would wager that it was just one of the composers who championed the cheese.

The instrumental synth pop cues are, to put it gently, like traveling music from some cornball television series. It's super-happy and simplistic pop music, like something you'd hear in the background of a television ad for kid's action figures. It feels like someone spent about five minutes working on the 'background music' because they knew it wasn't really important to sell GI Joe action playsets. Think of the theme song to *The A-Team* or *CHiPs*, and try to imagine this as the soundtrack to a medieval fantasy film. It just doesn't work at all. It's a jarring disconnect each and every time this music is heard. I saw *Ladyhawke* at an indie theater, and the audience giggled and groaned at the music.

A film like this needed a serious and emotional orchestral score, not some cartoonish music of the day. I can only imagine how revered this film could be if they had hired Ennio Morricone, Howard Shore, Tangerine Dream or John Williams for the job. I wish someone would release a version of *Ladyhawke* with just the orchestral score

for the entire film, because it's really good. It matches the atmosphere and compliments the story instead of detracting from it. Strangely, the dated keyboard music is primarily only used for the first 50 minutes of the film. The remaining 70 minutes are, thankfully, just the orchestral score. So if you can make it past the 50-minute mark, the movie feels more appropriately synced.

Legend, another 1985 fantasy film directed by Ridley Scott, had similar soundtrack issues. Renowned composer Jerry Goldsmith initially scored *Legend*. But after test screenings went poorly, Scott hired German electronic band Tangerine Dream to write a more contemporary score. A very similar situation happened with the 1972 Sam Peckinpah crime movie, *The Getaway*. Jerry Fielding, who had worked with Peckinpah numerous times, scored the film. But actor Steve McQueen had final cut of the film and he didn't like Fielding's score, so he hired Quincy Jones to create a jazzier score. In the alternative universe that I want to live in, Tangerine Dream would have been hired to score *Ladyhawke*.

But let's focus on my favorite part of the film, the climactic battle in the cathedral. We've seen Navarre kill lots of soldiers by this point and we know he is a skilled fighter with the noble motivation of love behind him. Clad in all black with a cape with red accents, riding on a black horse, wielding a black handled sword, he presents as the villain. While the actual villain, the Bishop, dresses in all white cloaks and hides inside his church chamber defended by dozens of loyal soldiers. Navarre has lots of showy hero moments - using his sword to swat his metal helmet face-shield down into place; standing atop a rocky summit shooting his crossbow; approaching a fearful soldier and swatting his sword away with only his gloved hand.

But when he finally enters the Bishop's cathedral during Mass to kill him, the intensity of the film is ramped up for the big finale. The sound of the horse's hooves clopping on the stones announces Navarre's arrival, but also announces the arrival of Marquet, the Captain of the Guard, there to defend the Bishop. The faces of the parishioners reflect the shock of this holy place being defiled by knights with swords bringing violence and bloodshed.

What I love about this fight is that it's messy and frenetic, like a real battle would be. It isn't the Hollywood version with perfect strikes and overly heroic moments. It begins as a jousting battle with each knight charging each other and striking with their swords. You can feel the heft of Navarre's sword just from watching him wield it. It's certainly not a light prop sword. A horse actually falls down to the cobblestones during the battle. I'm not entirely sure if it was an intentional stunt or an accident caught on film. They ride between the huge pillars, scattering people out of their way. The sound of the hooves and swords clattering on the cathedral bricks is unique. Marquet tackles Navarre off his horse and they fight on foot. They punch, kick and throw each other onto the walls in between sword strikes. Marquet throws his helmet at Navarre, breaking a stained-glass window. There are point-of-view shots from inside Navarre's helmet with the metal faceplate bars quartering the screen. More soldiers come out of the sidelines and attack Navarre as he tries to make his way towards the Bishop.

Something happens during the battle that leads Navarre to believe incorrectly that Isabeau is dead. So now he fights with a fury even greater than before, believing he has nothing left to lose or protect, and no reason to live himself. The nature of the battle gets more surreal here, with various sound effects being altered in the sound mix, adding extreme echoes and slowing down the sound itself. Both the visual images and audio effects are now in slow motion, which has a powerful affect on the viewer. This final confrontation is an almost fifteen-minute sequence of sustained action. It's honestly one of my favorite swordfights, easily surpassing other similar films like *Excalibur* and *Highlander*.

Ladyhawke is available on Warner Archive Collection Blu-Ray, which is a huge improvement over the previous DVD release.

Harold's Long, No Good, Very Bad Day
THE LONG GOOD FRIDAY

by Rachel Bellwoar

The opening credits for John Mackenzie's *The Long Good Friday* (1980) aren't flashy - it's just white text on a black background - but the film actually starts a moment earlier, when the screen is still black and 'Handmade Films Presents' hasn't appeared yet. That's the moment Francis Monkman's music starts - specifically the song *Taken* - and if it doesn't get under your skin right away, rest assured it will by the end of the movie. Monkman manages to capture the unrelenting pressure of the long Good Friday that Harold Shand (Bob Hoskins) is about to have in one repetitive, anxiety-inducing tune that never lets up.

The '80s would go on to rely on saxophone scores too much, but Monkman's theme starts the decade off right. His score for *The Long Good Friday* is a masterpiece. It's impossible to imagine the film without it.

There are a number of reasons why *The Long Good Friday* still stands as one of the greatest gangster (not to mention British) films of all time. A main one is Barrie Keeffe's screenplay. Forget the quotable lines (of which there are many, of course). Other gangster films have those, too. What Keeffe's screenplay does is dare to be overwhelming right from the opening sequence.

The first thing to recognize about *The Long Good Friday* is that it isn't a film to watch if you're half asleep. Even awake, there's a lot to take in and you have to be up for it. As the opening credits draw to a close the first thing we see is a house in the middle of the countryside. We'll return to this house a couple of times during the opening sequence, as a way of marking the passage of time as the sun goes down. From there, Mackenzie drops viewers in front of one of the windows, looking in from the outside at some men sitting at a table. Then there's a cut to a man carrying a suitcase, but his face remains out of frame, dehumanizing him and making the suitcase the focus. Later he will be identified as Harold's best friend, Colin (Paul Freeman), but for the moment he's just a guy who

winds up at a bar while the suitcase winds up with the men inside the house.

Then come the guns. Because Mackenzie has viewers looking into the house from the outside, the next part feels like a video game. Suddenly there's a gun smashing in through the window and viewers share the gunman's point of view. It's a moment that feels reminiscent of Bob Clark's *Black Christmas* (which opened with viewers sharing the killer's point of viewer) and it won't be the last time *The Long Good Friday* forecasts the slasher craze of the '80s.

Meanwhile, in the bar, Colin narrowly escapes being killed by some unknown assailants who were waiting for him in the parking lot (his driver [Leo Dolan] and the young man Colin was about to pick up [Kevin McNally] aren't so lucky). Mackenzie then moves the action to London, where we see the dead driver's coffin arriving by train. Again, at this point, it could be the driver or the young man's coffin - that information isn't confirmed until later, but it's all a matter of patience. No detail is accidental, and the degree to which Keeffe actually sets everything up in advance is truly remarkable, even though you only notice it after you've seen the film multiple times.

That's why it's so effective, though, because when the driver's widow (Patti Love) then shows up in the next scene and spits on a guy who we later learn is Harold's right-hand man, Jeff (Derek Thompson), it's conspicuous but easily forgotten. Later the widow comes back in a big way, but because Mackenzie and Keeffe allow so much time to pass (and so much happens in that time), her significance later comes as a surprise when it should've been a huge red flag.

As much as Mackenzie and Keeffe ask viewers to trust them, they also trust in the intelligence of the viewer to pay attention. There's not much handholding, but that's part of the satisfaction of watching the film - you have to work to understand what's going on. Mackenzie and Keeffe use the opening sequence to establish the atmosphere (the sense that somebody's always watching) and to train viewers on how to watch the film, stressing the importance of being observant. It's not enough to keep up with the conversation onscreen. You also have to clock the car that passes behind Jeff's shoulder. It's only because the camera follows the car that it's importance becomes apparent, but it's a teaching moment for what life is like in Harold's world. There's no letting your guard down. You have to notice *everything*.

The Long Good Friday is a gangster film, but it's also a mystery (and the reason mysteries are satisfying is because - at least in the fictional ones - all the pieces come together at the end). Instead of a detective, though, *The Long Good Friday* has Hoskins' Harold Shand, who has to figure out who is targeting his corporation when he's about to close a major deal with the Americans (represented by Eddie Constantine's Charlie). Fittingly, Shand's entrance into the film, while late, is memorable. Right before the close-up on his face, Mackenzie draws attention to a plane that's landing with British Airways written on the side. In a film that will go on to pit America against Britain, Shand represents Britain and in this opening scene he's back in London after a visit to New York, and preparing to schmooze Charlie. As Harold makes his way through Heathrow airport, Monkman's *Taken* returns for the second time, underlining Harold's importance but not yet coming across as the stressful anthem it will become later in the movie. That's because Harold doesn't know what's transpired while he's been away. He's completely unprepared for the chaos that's about to ensue.

Things quickly escalate from there, as a series of bombs start going off in places that are important to Harold's business. Then Colin, who managed to survive the parking lot hit, gets stabbed by Pierce Brosnan (making his feature film debut). This time, Monkman's synth music gives the scene a slasher feel, while there's also the salacious angle of the attack occuring during a forbidden gay tryst.

What offsets the somewhat uncomfortable, judgmental vibe of this sequence is Harold's visible grief when he learns his best friend has been murdered. He never once feels the need to clarify that he's straight or make sure that no one mistakes their friendship for romance. Harold has bigger fish to fry, but this is the beauty of Hoskins' performance. His Harold is completely secure in his masculinity. He's a man who isn't afraid to be emotional in public, who doesn't need to be stone-faced all the time to be frightening (and, boy, he *is* frightening). There's nothing scarier than Harold angry but he's also heartbreaking and hilarious, the whole package, the definition of a dynamic leading man.

The real beating heart of *The Long Good Friday*, though, is the relationship between Harold and his wife, Victoria

(Helen Mirren). During their first conversation in the film, he brings up that he's been divorced from his first wife for ten years. Ten years is a number that keeps coming up in relation to the length of time Harold has been able to keep the peace in London. We recongize a direct correlation between Harold's success and his marriage to Victoria.

Harold and Victoria don't just love each other, they're partners. And it shows in how much Victoria is involved in the corporation. When the bombings start and Harold has to leave to deal with the fallout, it's Victoria he entrusts with keeping the Americans occupied. No male escort to supervise. No driver. No checking in. Part of that, of course, could be chalked up to the fact that Harold is too busy to think about calling her, but the fact of the matter remains that this is the biggest deal he's ever made, and he doesn't hesitate about leaving his wife in charge.

It's not hard to understand why. Before any of the men in Harold's outfit, it's Victoria who's always by his side. The pub they were about to eat in explodes. It's Victoria who, without hesitation, joins him to help the survivors. At one point Harold is about to make a rash decision. It's Victoria who squares off with him, pushing the other men aside. Victoria isn't the Watson to Harold's Sherlock. She's the one who cracks the case, and Mirren never lets viewers forget it.

When Harold decides to go home and take a break from cleaning-up Friday's mess, it's a welcome reprieve from the action. Apparently, according to Mackenzie (whose commentary is included on Arrow's 2018 Blu-Ray release), it was originally supposed to be a sex scene. Instead, they are alone and, for the first time, Harold questions how Victoria's handled the Americans. What consolation might've been gleaned from the fact that he waited until they were in the privacy of their own home to express his doubts is broken the moment he pushes Victoria onto the couch, yet instead of becoming more violent, he shocks himself and immediately apologizes.

Watching this scene, in light of how Harold's sudden anger later results in another character ending up dead, adds some perspective, because it could've played out completely differently. It's not for nothing that Harold instantly regrets his actions and says so aloud, but that doesn't mean Victoria wasn't in danger. Both Hoskins and Mirren play the scene for all they've got, as their characters finally get a chance to react to the day's events and how close they came to being killed, but their marriage survives the altercation. There's even still a hint of sex in the fact that the next morning Harold is wearing the same robe Victoria was wearing the night before, but his abuse hangs over the rest of the movie until Monkman's *Taken* plays the film to a close.

Harold and Victoria Shand's fates may be sealed, but *The Long Good Friday* is immortal. Some people love *The Godfather* or *Goodfellas*. For my money, *The Long Good Friday* has them beat.

by Peter Sawford

There are certain films, classics if you like, which can be watched multiple times because the story and the characters are so multi-layered. Upon each viewing, you see and understand and appreciate something new. Then there are films you can watch dozens of times simply because they put a big, soppy grin on your face. *Big Trouble in Little China* (1986) is an example of the latter.

I have to admit that when it first came out it nearly passed me by. I was a John Carpenter fan, but I identified him as a master of horror (thanks to *Halloween* and *The Fog*) or gritty action films (like *Assault on Precinct 13* and *Escape from New York*). I wasn't sure *Big Trouble in Little China* would be my cup of tea. I eventually watched it at the insistence of a good friend, and was surprised to find myself loving every minute, from the opening shot of the Pork Chop Express thundering into view through to the final credits roll.

Truck driver Jack Burton (Kurt Russell) arrives in San Francisco's Chinatown in his rig, the Pork Chop Express, and meets up with his friend Wang Chi (Dennis Dun). But things start to spiral out of control when Wang and Jack go to the airport to meet Wang's fiancée (Suzee Pai). She is promptly kidnapped, pitching Wang and Jack into a battle against the power of a centuries-old sorcerer, David Lo Pan (James Hong), and his three bodyguards, the Storms - Thunder (Carter Wong), Rain (Peter Kwong) and Lightning (James Pax). Lo Pan was cursed after being defeated in battle, and only by marrying then sacrificing a green-eyed woman can the curse be lifted.

Wang's girlfriend is that rarest of creatures - a Chinese woman with green eyes. Jack and Wang are helped by a lawyer, Gracie Law (Kim Cattrall) - who was at the airport protecting a young migrant's civil rights - and a local mystic who doubles as a sightseeing tour guide named Egg Shen (Victor Wong).

In many respects, this was a strange film for Carpenter to make. Up to that point he'd been something of a one-man studio, working as writer, director, producer, often composer and occasional editor. *Big Trouble in Little China* marked a new approach for him in that it was made within the confines - constrictions possibly - of a major Hollywood studio. Moreover, it was a fantasy/martial arts/comedy/action hybrid, so far out of Carpenter's comfort zone that you wonder what inducements the studio must have thrown his way to get him to make it.

Despite mashing up genres, Carpenter approaches the task with absolute professionalism, very gently turning it into a loving parody of the Asian martial arts films that were finding a large audience in Europe and the United States at the time. He also fully embraces the anarchy and madness of the situations in the story. He lets his imaginations run riot and encourages his crew to do the same. A lot of credit must go to production designer John J. Lloyd, art director Les Gobruegge, set designers George R. Nelson and Rick Simpson, and cinematographer Dean Cundey (here collaborating with Carpenter for the final time). Between them, they create a universe where strange and bizarre monsters are commonplace, where buildings become labyrinthine mazes, where tunnels and ancient passageways run just feet below the streets of Chinatown, and where absolutely nothing ever seems quite as it should.

Carpenter sets out his stall from the word go, and we quickly become aware that, for the next 100 minutes, all bets are off - anything can, and probably will, happen. In the opening scene, Egg Shen sits in the District Attorney's office trying to explain events we're yet to see. The DA refuses to accept Egg's tale of magic and sorcery, so Egg produces electricity between his hands much to the DA's shock and amazement. Despite this slightly mystical opening, the next scenes suggest we might still be in standard Carpenter action film territory. Jack and Wang come face to face with a very real and much-feared Chinatown gang called the Lords of Death at the airport and then, after chasing them into the back streets of Chinatown, find themselves in the middle of a vicious fight between the Chang Sing and the far nastier Wing Kong.

So far, it all seems relatively normal for a martial arts actioner. But the introduction of the Storms and the apparition of David Lo Pan suddenly shifts us into a world of fantasy and magic. The Storms have supernatural powers as ascribed by their names and seem impervious to anything mere mortals can do. Lo Pan appears as a spectral figure who can withstand being run over by Jack's truck (much to Jack's disbelief) and it's at this point that Carpenter proves himself an inspired choice to helm the pic. A lesser director might have allowed the story to dissolve into the realm of complete make-believe, giving normal characters a sudden and jarring ability to do incredible and abnormal things. But Carpenter always keeps the story and the characters grounded, true to their roots, believable within the context of the movie. Yes, the characters have amazing adventures and witness amazing feats, but you always accept them within the story. Right at the centre of it all is Jack Burton, perfectly played by Russell.

Big Trouble in Little China was originally conceived as a western and only later was it changed to a modern setting. Elements of that original western background are borne out in Russell's performance. Jack is a blowhard whose mouth works five seconds ahead of his brain and is possibly braver than the rest of his body. On more occasions than he'd care to admit, he makes a wisecrack only to regret it seconds later when the full consequences hit home.

Jack is at his happiest driving his truck, espousing his philosophies through his CB radio where no-one can argue, complain or disagree with what he's saying. He has certainly been married more than once, and we get the impression that on each occasion his refuge was his truck - that when push came to shove, his love for his truck was always stronger. Indeed, it's his desire to get his truck back that really leads Jack to join the fight against Lo Pan and

his cohorts. Wang's fiancée's life may be in danger and Lo Pan may be on the cusp of lifting his curse and taking over the universe, but in Jack's eyes the Pork Chop Express has been stolen and somebody is going to pay!

Russell brilliantly taps into his inner John Wayne. But it's not a purebred incarnation of the Duke - it's a hybrid John Wayne, a John Wayne fused with a healthy dose of Wile E. Coyote. More often than not, Jack's moment of triumph, his chance to be the hero, is spoilt by either his innate ability to do something stupid or for circumstances to conspire to ruin things for him. That's why he knocks himself out just before a big fight starts, slips and falls into the water when a heroic dive is called for, gets stuck beneath the heavy corpse of a guard he's just killed, battles the bad guys while unknowingly smeared in lipstick, or selects the reverse gear when trying to make a fast frontal escape! If there's a wrong way to do something at the wrong time, you can bet on Jack to do it. He's an almost everyman hero. We can't all be a James Bond, but we can all be a Jack Burton - you just need the right amount of stubbornness and desire to do the right thing for your friends.

This was the fourth collaboration between Carpenter and Russell after *Elvis* (1979), *Escape from New York* (1981) and *The Thing* (1982) and it shows. There's a mutual trust and respect between them. Carpenter knows he can ask anything of Russell, and Russell knows that whatever Carpenter asks of him will be for the benefit of the film. Both grasp the inherent humour in the situation and Russell is more than happy to send up his Snake Plissken persona and end up looking the fool. Although top of the cast and the most central character, Jack is still a sort of sidekick to Wang Chi. It's Wang's desire to get his girlfriend back at any cost that drives the story. Wang finds endless reserves of courage in his quest and Dennis Dun clearly has

great fun quietly spoofing his only previous role in *Year of the Dragon* (1985).

Over the film Wang evolves from a hard-working restaurant owner with a dodgy gambling affliction into a fully-fledged martial arts hero capable of flying through the air while sword fighting, but always with a grin and an inner belief that he'll survive no matter what the odds. Originally the producers didn't want Kim Cattrall for the role of pain-in-the-ass, self-righteous lawyer Gracie Law due to her past performances in *Porky's* (1981) and *Police Academy* (1984), but eventually she won them over. Gracie is no simpering, screaming damsel-in-distress thrown in just for love interest. Cattrall makes her intelligent, brave, resourceful and more than happy to put herself into the middle of the action when necessary. It's only in her romantic interest in Jack that Gracie refuses to accept what's right in front of her face. From the moment they first meet at the airport, she refuses to fall for his easy charm and cheesy chat-up lines, and scoffs at the idea that he means anything to her. But her genuine distress when she thinks he hasn't made it out alive gives away her true feelings. Though you want them to end up together, it's more fitting that they both continue to deny what everyone else can plainly see.

The final piece of the jigsaw is Hong's inspired performance as Lo Pan. Whether he's a seven-foot apparition capable of gliding through walls, creating blinding lights from his fingertips, or balding, frail and wheelchair bound, Hong is endlessly watchable. He has a fantastic line in irritability when Jack gets a little too sassy for his liking.

The special effects are excellent. Sometimes they are like a caricature with an almost cartoonish quality. The set

for Lo Pan's wedding, with the stairway leading up to the grinning skull, is spectacular. The floating eyeball which acts as Lo Pan's spy is surely one of the nastiest CCTV's you'll ever see.

When the dust has settled, the bad guys have all been defeated and Jack is once again back on the road telling the world his life story, the door is left just open for a possible sequel. To date, this has never happened (though there have been graphic novels, endorsed by Carpenter, which move Jack Burton's adventures forward). In some ways, the lack of a sequel or two is a shame. The characters could have easily been transplanted to another time and place for further adventures. Having said that, it's not always possible to catch lightning in a bottle twice so perhaps leaving the film as a standalone is for the best. So many films have proved in the past that a poor sequel can knock the original off its much-loved perch.

Writing the script proved a somewhat tortuous affair, with Gary Goldman and David Z. Weinstein turning in the original screenplay with an 1880s western setting. When the studio decided on updating the story and bringing it into modern times, Goldman refused to do any re-writes and W. D. Richter was brought in to overhaul the entire story. Goldman and Weinstein complained, the Writers Guild of America sided with them, and Richter had to make do with an 'Adapted by' credit. This angered Carpenter, even though he'd made a number of additions to Richter's work himself.

Sadly, despite keeping up a great pace, having many great action sequences, and being full of humour and putting a warm feeling in the pit of our stomach, *Big Trouble in Little China* was a financial flop which divided critics. It only recouped $11m of its estimated $25m budget. While the normally irascible Harlan Ellison praised it to the skies, Roger Ebert seemed to miss the point entirely by stating that he didn't care about the characters and that there was no apology for stereotypes straight from a '40s Charlie Chan or Fu Manchu film. Carpenter and Russell blamed 20th Century Fox for not really knowing how to promote it. They felt the studio eventually gave up on it and opted to cut their losses (Russell did later admit it was a difficult film to market).

For Carpenter, the financial and critical failure combined with the behind-the-scenes problems, soured his attitude towards working within the studio system. He didn't

make a studio picture again until *Vampires* in 1998.

Big Trouble in Little China has always reminded me of the old action serials popular in American cinema of the '40s that used to be shown by the BBC in the late '70s. No matter what danger the hero might have found himself in, you always knew he'd find some way out no matter what the odds, and would end up defeating the bad guy and saving the girl. Jack Burton may not appear on many people's list of the great screen heroes of all time, but I'd have been more than happy to see him walking into my local bar, slamming his keys on the bar, ordering a beer and starting to tell everyone about his latest adventure.

Big Trouble in Little China and Jack Burton still rock, and the cinematic world is a better place thanks to them.

'80s Christmas Cheer

by Nic Parker

Whenever Halloween ends and we begin approaching the Christmas season at full throttle, I always find myself asking: "What's the greatest Christmas movie ever made?"

I'm sure some of you will instantly come up with Jimmy Stewart in *It's a Wonderful Life* (1946) or the Bing Crosby vehicle *White Christmas* (1954). Both are beloved classics which show up on television every year over the Yuletide period, but they are over sixty years old and don't reflect modern society. I tried to recall titles from the '60s and '70s, but couldn't come up with many films from that era which people might mention as must-sees for festive cheer. The 1970 musical version of *Scrooge* with Albert Finney, maybe, but that's about it.

I'm sure many of you would choose your top Christmas movie from one of the six iconic '80s films that I'll be discussing in this article.

There have been a few nice Christmas films between the '90s and now too, but I find they generally cater for a narrow target audience. Movies like Tim Allen's *Santa Clause* films, for example, which are a brilliant, fresh take, but are harmless family entries without a single swear word. *Love Actually* (2003), *The Holiday* (2006) and *Last Christmas* (2019) were big hits too, but their central themes revolved around love and relationships with added drama. Their tear-inducing stories cater more for grownups or those of us who love a good romance. The first two *Home Alone* films stand out a bit, as they knew how to cater for a wider audience; the same applies to the cheery Schwarzenegger fun fest *Jingle All the Way* (1996). Those three comedies remember to employ one of the

must-have ingredients of any successful Christmas movie: a gallery of oddball supporting characters.

Horror fans have had their fair share with films like *A Christmas Horror Story* and *Krampus*, but you'd hardly show either of those to your non-horror-loving relatives, right?

So, to find the greatest Christmas films, I recommend going back to the '80s - that magical time before an evil elf had invented the Hallmark Channel, with its interchangeable generic shit, repetitive stories, actors whose faces you forget within thirty seconds, and scripts which feel like they were concocted in ten minutes.

There's been a lot of nostalgia for the '80s since... well, actually, since that magical decade merged into the '90s. The music and the movies have stayed firm favourites, even among people who were born long after. The passion for the arts of that period continues to be passed on to younger generations.

In the '80s, the big Hollywood studios were still in the hands of people who came from a film background who knew what the magic of movies was all about. Script writers had a knack for creating that hectic, joyful, expectant December mood. They knew the essential component for an unforgettable Christmas movie (indeed, all movies) is to create great characters. They didn't just concentrate on the main characters, either - they always tossed in great supporting roles too: the oddball, the grumpy geezer, the sleazy neighbour, etc, each of whom contributed to make the film memorable. They knew crazy and hilarious elements would give people something to relate to and laugh at, and would make the film an annual must-watch whenever the festive season came around.

It's remarkable that four of the six films I'm about to examine feature, in main roles, comedians who were at the height of their game and fame - John Candy, for instance, who was one of the best exports from Canada ever, and a regular face in many comedies from the '70s until the early '90s (sadly, he suffered a fatal heart attack in 1994 at the untimely age of 43). There were Steve Martin, Bill Murray and Eddie Murphy too, all of whom remain quite active to this day. Or Dan Aykroyd and Chevy Chase, who we hardly ever see in movies these days. Aykroyd most recently appeared in the brilliant *Ghostbusters: Afterlife* (2021) but seems happy mostly concentrating on marketing his own vodka brand, Crystal Head. Chase always had a reputation for being a nightmare to work with, and his recent roles were more-or-less cameos in *Hot Tub Time Machine 2* (2015) and *Vacation* (2015), where he reprised his role as beloved Clark Griswold, father of the most chaotic family ever.

In fact, the Griswolds lead us right into the first Christmas classic from the '80s that I'd like to discuss. *National Lampoon's Christmas Vacation* (1989) invites us to enjoy the festive season with one of the most chaotic and loveable family of all time - lo and behold: the Griswolds!

The creator of the Griswolds, the fabulous John Hughes, was one of Hollywood's most prolific writers and directors and was taken from us tragically early in 2009, at only 59 years of age. Hughes not only created the Griswolds, he

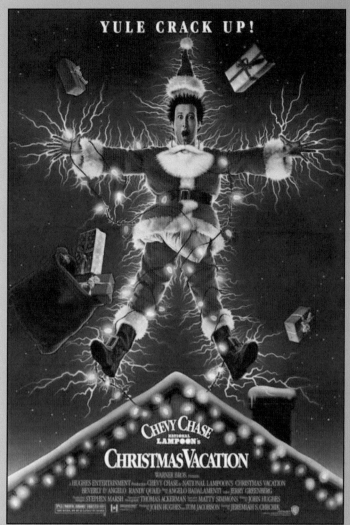

YULE CRACK UP!

CHEVY CHASE
NATIONAL LAMPOON'S
CHRISTMAS VACATION
WARNER BROS

was also behind the well-known and still much-loved *The Breakfast Club* (1985) and *Ferris Bueller's Day Off* (1986), as well as writing the first two *Home Alone* movies which were directed by Chris Columbus. His stories depicted the Griswolds and Kevin wreaking Christmas havoc, and he was also responsible for another iconic film that I'll be mentioning later in this feature - *Planes, Trains and Automobiles* (1987). Hughes understood people very well and knew how to write believable characters. Heartbreak, loss, grief, coming of age - he always added so much heart and soul to his films without ever making viewers retch because of treacle-soppy kitsch. It's only right that we remember him, and thank him for some of the greatest Christmas flicks ever.

Clark Griswold and family had already gained considerable fame thanks to the first *Vacation* movie. The follow-up *European Vacation* upped the ante, showing them wreaking havoc all over Europe, destroying old heritage sites while mother Ellen (Beverly D'Angelo) became an accidental porn star in Italy.

In *Christmas Vacation*, we catch up with the Griswolds as they prepare for the most wonderful time of the year. It's the classic division of duties - Clark decorates the house with any lights he can get his hands on, while Ellen is in charge of the food and gifts for the expected gathering of family members, wanted or unwanted. Clark is in festive mood and has already decided he will use his yearly bonus to fulfil his dream of building a swimming pool in the garden.

Christmas Vacation shows the funniest 'average' family get-together imaginable, not just by American standards but valid worldwide (which surely added to its huge success). We recognise the set-up only too well - grandparents who are as grumpy as Scrooge, not to mention hard-of-hearing or halfway senile; Ellen having to put up with endless criticism from judgmental grandmas; the kids dreading having to keep their great-cousins entertained; Clark feeling overwhelmed when his run-down cousin Eddie appears uninvited in his campervan with his family and their snot-spraying Rottweiler. Randy Quaid gives a memorable performance as Eddie, delivering a lot of iconic quotes. "Shitter is full," he declares when emptying the contents of the camping mobile's septic tank into the sewer (needless to say, the later consequences are gloriously unforgettable).

The character of Cousin Eddie, as well as the two arrogant yuppie neighbours Margo and Todd (Julia Louis-Dreyfus and Nicholas Guest), are perfect examples of why supporting characters matter so very much. They are the rich and stylish modern couple unfazed by all the Christmas craziness, and the story casts them as accidental victims of Clark's general clumsiness as their household is slowly destroyed - much to the glee of the viewer.

Ellen does what all mothers do, trying to fit everyone in and make all of them comfortable. But of course, everything that can go wrong will go wrong - delighting us, the viewers, as we suddenly realise our own dreaded family Christmas party isn't that bad after all.

While the family braves one catastrophe after another, Clark finally has a breakdown when he receives an envelope containing what he expects to be the cheque with his yearly bonus. Instead, he finds his boss has sent him nothing but a shitty subscription.

Cousin Eddie realises how much this gratification means to Clark and now makes it his personal task to save Christmas. He sets out with his fucked-up camping mobile and kidnaps Clark's boss, who then gets an earful from Clark about the spirit of Christmas and what workers expect from their superiors, emphasized by scornful looks from the gathered family. (This is an essential scene, as valid today as it was back then.) Just as Clark's boss begins to understand that Christmas is the season to be giving, all hell breaks loose when a SWAT team hit the Griswold household with full force.

Christmas Vacation has all the Christmas vibe you need, but instead of a sweet and romantic story it offers festive family madness at its very best. The characters lean hard into the realm of crazy and grotesque. Its comedy moments rely on various elements, with a strong emphasis on slapstick and chance moments, and never fail to hit the mark. One of the forgotten tricks of the trade in comedy is the 'Running Gag', which is depicted beautifully here with Clark trying to make the Christmas lights around the house finally work and inadvertently ruining the relationship - and house - of the couple next door by being generally as clumsy as hell. Chevy Chase is the epitome of the stressed father on the verge of a nervous breakdown and the film is a thing of sheer comic beauty that you'll want to revisit every year.

The '80s saw a good run of Christmas horror movies, with shockers like *Christmas Evil* (1980), *Don't Open till Christmas* (1984) and *Elves* (1989), etc. There was also the *Silent Night, Deadly Night* series which ran to three films within a single decade. But it's Joe Dante's ingenious *Gremlins* (1984) which surely has to be the most successful and memorable Christmas horror of the era. *Gremlins* remains a rare beast - festive entertainment for the whole family, creepy enough to call a horror movie but funny and tame enough to watch with the kids.

An inventor of silly and mostly useless things, Randall Peltzer (Hoyt Axton), little suspects what havoc a super-cute Mogwai will wreak on his hometown when he buys the creature from an old Chinaman as a Christmas present for his son Billy (Zach Galligan). As soon as Randall gets home, Billy is enchanted by the curious Mogwai which he names Gizmo. Gizmo is a unique, loveable pet that anyone would love to own, but he comes with certain instructions - he must be kept out of direct sunlight, must never become wet, and should never, ever be fed after midnight.

One of the variations of horror is, and always has been, the cautionary tale and here we have it in the form of how to meticulously take care of an exotic animal. As expected, Billy fails to follow all the instructions. A splash of water hits little Gizmo and not only does it cause the Mogwai great pain, but little fur balls start popping out of him. These fur balls eventually become other Mogwai. Gizmo's 'offspring' are not as well-behaved as the little cute guy. Indeed. they are born mischief-makers. The most intelligent of them, called Stripe (because of a

fluffy white tuft of fur on his head), strives for them to become something else entirely. And soon, all the Mogwai except Gizmo turn into Gremlins, vicious little demonic monsters, a living, breathing mix of lizard and action figure. The nefarious bunch cause damage all over town, causing havoc and playing mean tricks on everyone, and it's up to Billy and his girlfriend Kate (Phoebe Cates) to try to outsmart Stripe and his growing bunch of Gremlins.

Dante's fabulous creatures - the uber-cute Gizmo and the mischievous critters led by the nefarious Stripe - became instant stars with movie fans. To this day, they rake in millions of dollars as new merchandising items continue to be produced.

Billy's girlfriend Kate, portrayed by '80s babe Cates, has her own sad story about why she hates Christmas which is as brilliant as it is funnily gruesome. Look too for young Corey Feldman as a kid from the neighbourhood, and one of the best characters, the clearly grumpy resolute neighbour Mr. Futterman, played by genre favourite Dick Miller. Miller was a friend of director Dante and starred in over 180 productions prior to his death. Futterman was such a fan favourite that he reappeared in *Gremlins 2* (1990) where he helped save the day once more.

There has been some talk during recent years that Dante might helm a third *Gremlins* entry, but to date no definite sequel has been announced.

Bill Murray rose to superstar fame with *Ghostbusters* (1984), and before the sequel hit theatres, he starred as Frank Cross in *Scrooged* (1988). Instead of doing another period version of the Charles Dickens classic, this fresh take keeps all the key elements but sets the story in a modern-day television network, with Murray playing ruthless manager Frank Cross. Cross is cynicism personified and only believes in success and money. His show is filled with scantily clad dancers and whatever else he can think of to guarantee high ratings on Christmas Eve. He doesn't care if his employees would rather spend Christmas with their families; he expects them to work as hard as he does. Cross doesn't even mind firing people on Christmas Eve if they disagree with him. Among them is timid Eliot Loudermilk (Bobcat Goldthwait), a decision that will later backfire in the true sense of the word.

The Ghost of Christmas Present (Carol Kane) appears to Frank, giving him a hard time and treating him roughly, but Frank just shrugs off this event as a bad dream. Cross doesn't think he failed as a human and goes about business as usual, but when his ex-girlfriend Claire (the wonderful Karen Allen) steps on the scene, we learn that Frank was a completely different person back when he was in love. As his past decisions and his relationship with Claire are shown, we truly get to know the other, 'better' Frank and, after much confusion and heartbreak, there is the expected wonderful Christmas-for-all ending.

Murray excels as heartless Frank and has enough scenes for the usual Murray shenanigans. Fortunately, the documented quarrels between him and director Richard Donner are nowhere to be noticed on screen. Murray has a chronic reputation for being complicated to say the least, and despite countless feuds with directors and/or co-stars over the years, his performances have always been spot-on and he has remained a firm fan favourite right up to recent times.

Kane is all evil cheer, like a fairy on speed, as the Ghost of Christmas Present. Apparently, she didn't like having to manhandle Murray and, during one scene, accidentally caused Murray's lip to split causing a few days' production delay.

One of the essential characters is played by the wonderful funny-man Goldthwait. He came to fame in the '80s as

croaky-voiced crook-turned-cop Zed in *Police Academy 2, 3* and *4*. He's perfectly cast as shy employee Eliot, who gets fired on Christmas Eve by Frank and becomes so angry and devastated that he gets a shotgun and tries to kill Frank. These scenes make for some of the funniest in the film.

Scrooged, like the original Dickens story, endures as one of the great Christmas classics. It's been many peoples' favourite since it first hit theatres.

Trading Places (1983) offers a wonderful innuendo as a title. On one hand, it uses the stock market as one of its main settings; on the other, it gives us two very different characters being forced to trade their places in society.

Small-time crook Billy Ray Valentine (Eddie Murphy) cons people on the streets by faking that he's an invalid. Meanwhile, big financial player Louis Winthorpe III (Dan Akroyd) has it all - a NY mansion, an arm-candy fiancée, a butler, and more money than he could ever dream of. One evening, Winthorpe's employers - the brothers Randolph and Mortimer Duke (Ralph Bellamy and Don Ameche) - wager a simple bet and decide to trade the places of Billy Ray and Louis.

Winthorpe is slandered and ends up in jail, where everything points out to him being a drug dealer. He gets a lucky break when alley cat Ophelia (Jamie Lee Curtis), who was paid to con him, takes pity on him. Winthorpe enters the premises of his old company disguised as Santa Claus, drunk to his eyeballs, and, in one of the greatest moments in the film, sits on a bus and pulls from his filthy Santa costume a huge salmon which he stole from the company buffet. He takes a bite, chewing not only the fish but also his dirty fake Santa beard. He tries - and fails - to shoot himself, in a scene simultaneously heart-breaking and very funny, balancing the situation perfectly.

Meanwhile Billy Ray is not the crook the brothers expected him to be, proving himself quite useful at the stock market just by knowing how ordinary people think. Billy Ray eventually gets wind of how the two Dukes have used him and Winthorpe as playballs in their own wicked game. Together, with the help of Ophelia and butler Coleman (Denholm Elliott, in a part perfect for him), they work out a plan to ruin the rich old brothers.

Trading Places has all the quality ingredients of that era. Director John Landis was at the height of his fame. Eddie Murphy (on the verge of his *Beverly Hills Cop* heyday) and Dan Aykroyd (on the verge of his *Ghostbusters* heyday) make a fabulous team, and the two rich old gits are played by Hollywood royalty, Don Ameche and Ralph Bellamy, whose careers started in the '30s. Even Frank Oz turns up in a great cameo.

The story starts shortly before Christmas and the showdown takes place during the New Year celebrations on a train, with Jim Belushi in a small key role as a guy in a gorilla costume who is desperate to party. It's just a feelgood classic with perfect casting and scenes that are uproariously funny no matter how many times you've seen them.

I'd now like to turn towards one of the most heart-warming Christmas-style movies ever, though in reality it's set in the days and hours leading up to Thanksgiving, a holiday only celebrated in few countries outside the United States. *Planes, Trains and Automobiles* (1987) has the festive vibe and the essential elements of any good Christmas movie, and therefore I'm going to bend the rules to include it in this list.

The concept of the 'odd couple' was used in many movies of the '80s and proved a perfect recipe for action, fun and countless hilarious scenes. The initial premise of two totally different characters having to team up for some reason or other had been used splendidly in *Trading Places*, and is repeated to sheer perfection in *Planes, Trains and Automobiles*, which features two icons of comedy - the beloved late John Candy and Steve Martin - as two men who couldn't be more different.

Neal (Martin) wants nothing more than to get back home to his family in time for Thanksgiving, which proves very difficult when faced with heavy snowstorms, cancelled/overbooked flights and a series of unexpected disasters. At one point, he is taken to his rental car by bus only to find the car isn't where it's supposed to be. He has to walk all the way back to the terminal in the cold and snow - his four-lettered rant at the female agent (Edie McClurg) at the desk is an unforgettable scene of comedy gold.

To his aid comes jolly salesman Del (Candy) who is a man of many talents. He sees it as his crusade to stop at nothing to make sure his newly proclaimed best friend Neal get home for Thanksgiving. Trouble is, Neal finds Del irritating, overbearing and an all-round pain in the ass. This is just the start of many ridiculous situations, and incredibly well-crafted laugh-out-loud-moments, as they embark on an odyssey across the USA.

Planes, Trains and Automobiles at times makes us cringe as Neal and Del get into ever crazier situations. We empathise with Neal who seems on the brink of a nervous breakdown, but we see his flaws and frustrations too. Gradually, we come to see what a wonderful and generous person Del is, that he has the warmest heart beneath his

clumsy exterior and only wants to help.

The film has one of the sweetest endings ever. When we learn why Del doesn't need to be home for Thanksgiving and why he has persevered in helping Neal through every mishap and misadventure, most viewers will surely find themselves shedding a tear or two.

It is written, produced and directed by master craftsman John Hughes, and his influence clearly shows. The characters are brilliant and we, the viewers, develop genuine love for them during the running time. So, technically not a Christmas film, but *Planes, Trains and Automobiles* feels very much like one. It should be sought at once by anyone who has never seen it, and rewatched annually by anyone who knows it already.

Let's end this article with a bang - actually, quite a lot of bangs, explosions and shootouts.

Those of you shouting: "*Die Hard* is not a Christmas movie!" from the cheap seats, sit the hell down! Expect to be taken away by Krampus soon if you refuse to accept that it's one of THE quintessential Christmas movies of the '80s, indeed of all time!

New York policeman John McClane (Bruce Willis) arrives at LAX airport to spend Christmas with his kids and his wife Holly (Bonnie Bedelia). He's picked up by a limousine driver Argyle (De'voreaux White), courtesy of the company where Holly holds an important position. For McClane, it's an important visit - he and Holly have become estranged by the many miles between them, and he hopes to rekindle things with her. The Christmas party is in full swing at Nakatomi Tower when he arrives, and Holly is obliged take part, so she leaves him in her office

with its adjoining bathroom to freshen up. Security is low - it's Christmas Eve and soon everyone will be heading home. This is the perfect opportunity for Hans Gruber (Alan Rickman) and his men to enter the building, killing the few watchmen and locking down the premises. The terrorists have chosen their moment precisely, knowing there'll be little resistance but plenty of hostages for the taking. McClane doesn't even have time to get fully dressed after hearing gunshots and quickly assessing the new situation.

In his wifebeater vest and barefoot, it's only him against a whole bunch of terrorists. McClane flees further up, floor by floor, snatching a walkie-talkie from one of the bad guys and trying to call in the hijacking so that the cops know what exactly is going on in the building. Office Al Powell (Reginald VelJohnson) is near the premises and goes to check things out. Everything seems quiet to him… until, well, until all hell breaks loose! What follows is one of the most entertaining and action-packed two hours in movie history. Its 130 minute-plus runtime feels like 90 minutes or less.

Die Hard (1988) does everything right. It's like a textbook on how to make the perfect action movie, with added festive elements. There's buddy content too (a key element of so many of the films I've discussed in this article), with Powell and McClane starting to confide in each other over the radio waves.

Die Hard marked Bruce Willis's breakthrough as one of Hollywood's leading action stars after his role as a sly detective in the long-running TV series *Moonlighting*.

Alan Rickman was already well known in the UK, but his role as terrorist leader Hans Gruber paved the way for him to make it big away from his home country, specifically in Hollywood. His iconic role as the Willis' adversary was the beginning of a great career. Taken by pancreatic cancer in 2016, he is sorely missed in today's productions. A most wonderful actor, he could plays good guys or bad guys… but his baddies are legendary.

The casting is perfect right down to the smaller parts - Holly's cokehead colleague Ellis (Hart Bochner); the terrorist bunch; Argyle the limo driver who helps to save the day; the gung-ho FBI agents Big Johnson and Little Johnson (Robert Davi and Grand L. Bush).

Stephen E. de Souza and Jeb Stuart's script helps to bring a terrific version of Roderick Thorpe's novel 'Nothing Lasts Forever' to the screen, and the icing on the cake is having action specialist John McTiernan in the directing chair. *Die Hard* was such a hit that

it spawned four sequels (part two and three are great movies in their own right, but the quality fades a bit and over-the-top effects take precedence in the fourth and fifth instalments). Of the many great roles Willis has had, he will always be best remembered as hard as nails NY cop John McClane.

You can even buy Xmas sweatshirts with 'Ho! Ho! Ho! - Now I have a machine gun' printed on them (a nod to one of the coolest scenes in the movie). Every December, the internet is awash with memes saying: "It's not Christmas until Hans Gruber falls from Nakatomi Tower." As if you connoisseurs needed any more proof that *Die Hard* is a Christmas movie!

As I fade out this article, ho-ho-hopefully I've put you in the right spirit to face the annual Christmas frenzy. Cheer your spirits and fire up your Blu-ray players for some ultimate festive joy brought to you straight from the glorious '80s.

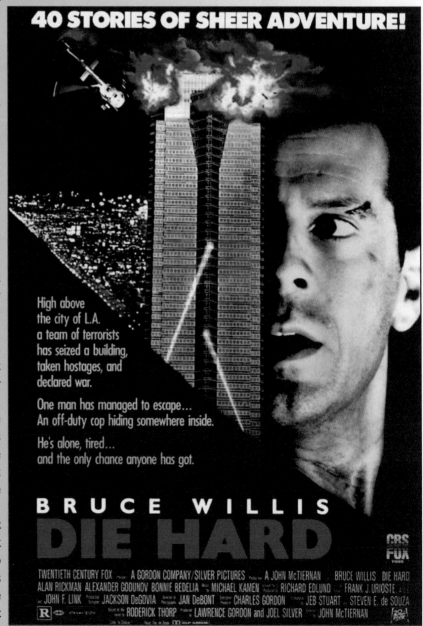

Dr. Andrew C. Webber investigates Norman Jewison and the art of collaboration.

AGNES OF GOD

For a film with few admirers, *Agnes of God* (1985) comes with a surprisingly good pedigree.

For one thing, it's directed by Norman Jewison who, when we look back on his filmography, is one of those overlooked journeymen (a bit like Stuart Rosenberg, Sydney Pollack and Richard Fleischer) who made a significant number of interesting and sometimes great movies in the latter half of the 20th century. He is responsible for, amongst others, Steve McQueen's gambling drama *The Cincinnati Kid* (1965), the brilliant Oscar-winning racial thriller *In the Heat of the Night* (1967), the slick heist movie *The Thomas Crown Affair* (1968), the musicals *Fiddler on the Roof* (1971) and *Jesus Christ Superstar* (1973), the cult sci-fi sports movie *Rollerball* (1975), the political drama *F.I.S.T* (1978) and Al Pacino's largely forgotten (but quite good) legal thriller *...And Justice for All* (1979). In the '80s he made the Burt Reynolds/Goldie Hawn comedy *Best Friends* (1982) and the racially themed whodunnit *A Soldier's Story* (1984) before tackling another theatrical adaptation with *Agnes of God*. He would go on to score one of the biggest hits of the decade, *Moonstruck* in 1987.

By anyone's standards, Jewison had an impressive filmography. That said, it's difficult to argue he was worthy of the *auteur* label (it's hard to discern any overall theme in his work other than his tendency to focus on outsiders). He moved effortlessly from thrillers to romances and from dystopian fantasies to musicals - making well-crafted and popular films for over 50 years - but he bowed out with the lacklustre Michael Caine spy drama *The Statement* in 2003.

Then there's the stars.

Jane Fonda (now in her 40s and looking increasingly like her dad) was still a major box office draw at the beginning the decade. Her '80s run began with the smash hit feminist comedy *9 to 5* (1980) which she followed with *On Golden Pond* (1981) wherein she acted alongside her father Henry to much acclaim. Next, she returned to working with Alan J. Pakula - who had directed her major breakthrough film *Klute* (1971) - on the excellent financial cataclysm thriller *Rollover* (1981). However, in *Agnes of God* she gives a rather wooden performance, marking a downturn in her popularity. She 'retired' from acting at the end of the '80s after a series of flops, among them the murder-mystery *The Morning After* (1986). She returned to the screen for *Monster-in-Law* (2005), presumably when the profits from her famous workout videos - so popular in the '80s and

'90s - began to dry up.

In *Agnes of God*, Fonda finds herself working alongside the extremely capable Anne Bancroft (*The Graduate*'s Mrs Robinson herself) who'd kicked off the '80s with a small but memorable role in David Lynch's *The Elephant Man* (1980) before acting alongside her husband Mel Brooks in the less-than-successful Lubitsch remake *To Be or Not to Be* (1983). She received a Best Actress Academy Award nomination for her role in *Agnes of God*, turning in a compelling performance but ultimately losing to Geraldine Page for the utterly forgettable *Trip to the Bountiful*.

Third on the bill in this 'woman's picture' is Meg Tilly, who'd been notable in both the belated Hitchcock sequel *Psycho 2* and Lawrence Kasdan's *The Big Chill* (both 1983). She is especially excellent here and was also nominated for an Oscar in the Supporting Actress category, losing out to Anjelica Huston for *Prizzi's Honour*. Tilly went on to appear in Milos Forman's *Valmont* (1989), *The Two Jakes* (1990) and the third version of *(Invasion of) The Body Snatchers* (1993) before retiring from acting. At this point she was having an affair with none other than Colin Firth. She is now a well-respected author.

Agnes of God is adapted from a play by John Pielmeier and revolves around the death of a baby, born under mysterious circumstances in a wintry Montreal convent. Is or isn't the

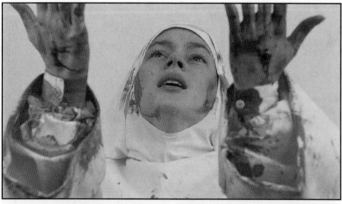

infant the product of an immaculate conception? Tilly is convincing as the child's 'innocent' mother - a novice nun who also shows signs of stigmata. Fonda plays a chain-smoking psychiatrist investigating the case and Bancroft is the mother superior who hopes to cover up the scandal. To say they don't make 'em like this anymore is a serious understatement.

In many ways - dealing as it does with the topics of faith, frustrated longings and female repression - *Agnes of God* fits into a long tradition of films featuring nuns, including the likes of Powell and Pressburger's *Black Narcissus* (1947), Audrey Hepburn's finest hour *The Nun's Story* (1959), Ken Russell's provocative *The Devils* (1971), Pawlikowski's recent and superb *Ida* (2013) and Paul Verhoeven's sexed-up *Benedetta* (2021) which was an obvious example of the softcore nunsploitation sub-genre.

Unfortunately, Jewison's film fails to fully capitalise on its unusual subject matter and includes a slightly hokey plot (replete with secret passages and some cod psychiatry) and the open ending (with a bolted-on narration by Fonda) spoils it. There's no real resolution and, although the movie certainly takes on big subjects (abuse, sexuality, motherhood, miracles, etc.), it fails to really say much about any of them. That's a pity since there's so much good work going on behind the camera.

The cinematography, for example, is by the great Sven Nykvist (aka 'Bergman's cameraman') who, as well as shooting some of Ingmar's most celebrated movies

(winning Oscars for both *Cries and Whispers* and *Fanny and Alexander*), found himself drawn to Hollywood - where he was responsible for some very good work in the '80s. He shot Bob Rafelson's neo-noir *The Postman Always Rings Twice* (1981), Bob Fosse's hard-to-see and rather tawdry *Star 80* (1983) and Woody Allen's *Another Woman* (1988) and *Crimes and Misdemeanours* (1989). He also photographed Phil Kaufman's excellent *The Unbearable Lightness of Being* (1988), for which he was nominated for a third Oscar, losing out, surprisingly, to *Mississippi Burning*. In *Agnes of God*, he shoots the austere convent and the actresses' faces with the same attention to detail he brought to his work with Bergman, albeit with one or two symbolic doves too many for my liking.

Outstanding cinematography is something most movie-goers can appreciate. However, the significance of well-edited sequences is a little harder to pin down, and editors are rarely celebrated despite their contribution being absolutely integral to the impact of the finished product. Of course, there are always exceptions - the work of Dede Allen on *Bonnie and Clyde* (1967), or editor-turned-director-turned-coke addict Hal Ashby who won an Oscar for editing Jewison's *In the Heat of the Night* (1967), or even Verna Fields' contribution to *Jaws* (1975). While nowhere near as well-known as any of them, the British editor Antony Gibbs - who edited *Agnes of God* - has a stunning resumé by any standards (and yet, shamefully, I had to look him up to learn about him as his name was unfamiliar to me).

Gibbs began his career during the so called British New Wave of the '60s (that's the bit before it got swinging, though Gibbs was there for that too). He edited *A Taste of Honey* (1961), *The Loneliness of the Long Distance Runner* (1962) *Tom Jones* (1963), *The Knack… and How to Get It* (1965) plus Nic Roeg's cult thriller *Performance* (1970). He worked with Roeg again on *Walkabout* (1971), both films being prime examples of how narratives can be shaped by the decisions editors make. In the '70s, he appeared to have become Jewison's go-to cutter, and together they made *Fiddler on the Roof*, *Jesus Christ Superstar* and *Rollerball*. He also found time to edit (among others) Don Siegel's *The Black Windmill* and Dick Lester's bomb-on-a-boat disaster movie *Juggernaut* in 1974, Richard Attenborough's star-laden war movie *A Bridge Too Far* (1977), and John Irvin's mercenary thriller *The Dogs of War* in 1980. Before *Agnes of God*, Gibbs had the almost impossible task of adding some sort of coherence to David Lynch's great folly *Dune* (1984). He failed, of course.

That notwithstanding, Gibbs brings real fluidity to *Agnes of God*. While its plot may well feel clunky, the images themselves are effectively composed and ordered with a number of montage sequences of the nuns at work (and especially one of them ice skating) proving particularly memorable.

Another key contributor is the prolific French composer Georges Delerue who, in the '80s, had previously scored Ulu Grosbard's crime drama *True Confessions* (1981) starring the two great Roberts, De Niro and Duvall, *The Black Stallion Returns* (1983) and Mike Nichols' *Silkwood* (1983). He'd go on to do good work for Oliver Stone later in the decade, writing the music for both *Salvador* and *Platoon* in 1986. The strings used throughout the *Agnes of God* soundtrack are an obvious precursor to his work on *Platoon*.

Delerue's Oscar nominated score for *Agnes of God* (John Barry's music for *Out of Africa* won) is another of the highlights, as is the production design (replete with *Vertigo*-style bell tower) which was the work of Ken Adam (of James Bond, Harry Palmer, *Dr Strangelove* and *Barry Lyndon* fame). The majority of the film was shot on location, but the convent's studio interiors are impeccably designed (as you'd expect from someone with Adam's reputation) and there is a real sense that this is a lived-in space which also reflects its inhabitants' beliefs, austerity and sense of community.

Agnes of God is hardly a lost classic but it *is* a film which deserves to be more widely known.

Sure, it's a bit of a one-off, but if you're looking for something small-scale which is not quite the sum of its parts but at least *tries* to do something unique, then it most definitely fits the bill. It's certainly a good example of how film remains a collective art form. Often, the best directors are those who know *exactly* with whom they want to work - the exact actors, the exact crew - and that's something Jewison appears to understand implicitly.

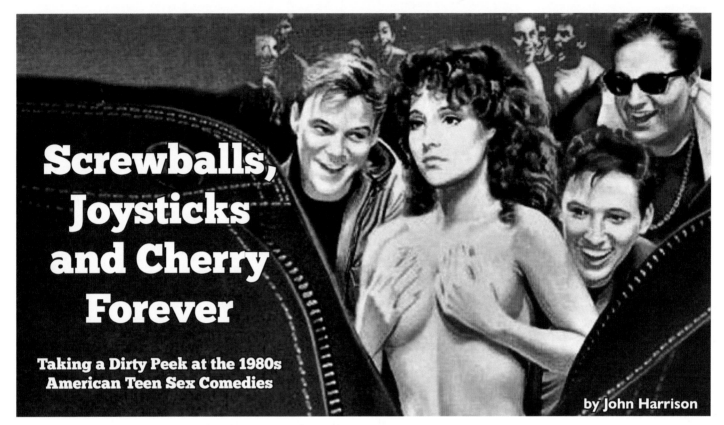

Screwballs, Joysticks and Cherry Forever

Taking a Dirty Peek at the 1980s American Teen Sex Comedies

by John Harrison

The American exploitation cinema landscape of the early '80s was dominated by two distinct genres. There were the slasher films, which had been introduced for a modern audience with *Halloween* (1978) before really exploding with the success of *Friday the 13th* (1980), and there were the teen sex comedies. Like the slasher movies, the teen sex comedies of the '80s also found their spark in the previous decade, with the release of John Landis' *Animal House* (1978), set in the '60s and inspired by stories written by Chris Miller for the humour magazine 'National Lampoon' (who co-produced the film).

Though a huge commercial hit (it was the highest-grossing comedy in America until topped by *Ghostbusters* in 1984), it took another film released three years later to really establish the teen sex comedy as a popular trend. *Porky's* (1981), like *Animal House*, also leaned into nostalgia by being set in 1954, but it significantly amped up the sex and sleaze factors and established a template for the genre that would be followed for the remainder of the decade.

It's no coincidence that the success and popularity of the teen sex comedies coincided with the start of the home video boom. Like many of the slasher films from the same period, it was on video where the teen sex comedies really found their audience during that peak 1982-1987 period. They provided the perfect fodder for that hungry generation that haunted their local video store in search of some undemanding silliness with a touch of titillation. Something to watch with beer, pizzas and bongs.

It's important at this point to establish some of the guidelines that separate a teen sex comedy from the more general teen comedy, or the romantic dramadies

from John Hughes which found a large audience during the '80s. Movies like *Fast Times at Ridgemont High* (1982, covered in 'Cinema of the '80s' #1) and *Risky Business* (1983) certainly placed a substantial emphasis on sexual activity, and may have contained nudity, but there was a lot more drama and depth to them than just the lead characters' dogged pursuit of sexual thrills . The teen sex comedy kept its mind (and other parts) firmly in the gutter and filled its films with an endless barrage of playground-level double entendre, and characters with names like Hugh G. Rection and Purity Busch. Invariably, there will also be a stern school dean, an obnoxious jock, totally clueless parents, an annoying younger sibling, and a bumbling nerd who often ends up scoring the best sex of the lot. Oh, and let's not forget an abundance of gratuitous T&A and fumbling sex that's usually over within seconds.

It all provided the cocktail of ingredients for a genre that has been despised by most critics over the years, and certainly for valid reasons. They can be tough to defend, and certainly need to be watched with an acceptance, or at least knowledge, of the less politically correct times in which they were made. For myself, they provide a sentimental bridge to a past that is fading ever more quickly, and I'm not ashamed to admit that many of them still make me laugh, even if it is at nothing more but their sheer, glorious stupidity.

"You'll be glad you came!"

As already noted, *Porky's* was the movie that really set the tone for what was to follow. Written and directed by Bob Clark, who had earlier impressed with his cult

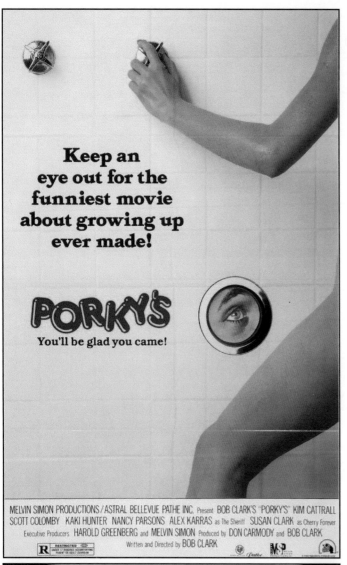

Keep an eye out for the funniest movie about growing up ever made!

PORKY'S

You'll be glad you came!

MELVIN SIMON PRODUCTIONS / ASTRAL BELLEVUE PATHE INC. Present BOB CLARK'S "PORKY'S" KIM CATTRALL SCOTT COLOMBY KAKI HUNTER NANCY PARSONS ALEX KARRAS as The Sheriff SUSAN CLARK as Cherry Forever Executive Producers HAROLD GREENBERG and MELVIN SIMON Produced by DON CARMODY and BOB CLARK Written and Directed by BOB CLARK

horror slasher *Black Christmas* (1974) and the Sherlock Holmes mystery thriller *Murder by Decree* (1979), *Porky's* was produced for less than five million dollars, and would go on to gross over $100 million in the United States alone, and nearly half of that again in overseas markets. I remember seeing *Porky's* twice at the Capitol Theatre in Melbourne when it was first released in Australia, one of the earliest R-rated movies I snuck into underage to see. Both sessions were jam packed and the theatre rocked from the constant uproars of laughter from the audience (including me and the school mates I went with). It really was a box-office phenomenon, becoming something of a must-see amongst that older teen and young adult demographic, and it's not hard to see why so many independent filmmakers were keen to exploit and cash in on its success.

Set in 1954 Florida, Clark first conceived the idea for *Porky's* in 1972, and based the story on his own experiences attending high school in that state. In the film, Edward 'Pee Wee' Morris (Dan Monahan) and his group of high school friends, frustrated by their failed attempts to get laid, decide to head to a hot spot in the Everglades called Porky's, a seedy strip club where it's rumoured that sexual favours can be bought. But when the large, and imposing, owner of the club, 'Porky' Wallace (Chuck Mitchell), instead cons the kids out of their money and then humiliates them by dunking them into the bayou to the amusement of his seasoned regulars, Pee Wee and his gang concoct a plan to raze Porky's club as revenge.

Naturally, the plan to take down Porky is drawn out by the addition of various sub-plots and set-pieces, most of which revolve around the teens and their comically disastrous pursuits of sex. A visit to a mature hooker named Cherry Forever (Susan Clark) descends into chaos when her enraged husband shows up wielding a machete, chasing the terrified and naked teens into the Everglades (though it turns out to be a prank). There are also a number of confrontations with stern female sports

coach Beulah Balbricker (Nancy Parsons), and a running gag involves the younger, beautiful coach Lynn Honeywell (Kim Cattrall in an early role), and the reason why she is referred to as 'Lassie'.

To its credit, *Porky's* does have a degree of substance to it, something you would expect coming from Bob Clark. The one serious sub-plot in the movie involves teen Tim Cavanaugh (Cyril O'Reilly) and his relationship with his father (Wayne Maunder), a volatile and racist ex-con who publicly abuses and belittles Mickey for losing a schoolyard fight to a Jewish boy. In fact, Tim has already developed antisemitism thanks to his brother's influence, though he predictably does develop acceptance and kinship with the Jewish boy in the group. This angle not only helps give *Porky's* some grounding and depth amongst all its outrageous antics, but provides a reminder that racism in '50s and '60s America, especially down south, was all-pervasive and went beyond simple black and white.

Setting the film in the '50s no doubt helped give *Porky's* an extra appeal. The bawdy humour and T&A quotient brought in the expected teen audiences (mostly males), while the '50s backdrop gave it a layer of *American Graffiti* (1973) and *Happy Days* nostalgia, which attracted the older audiences who had come of age during that time.

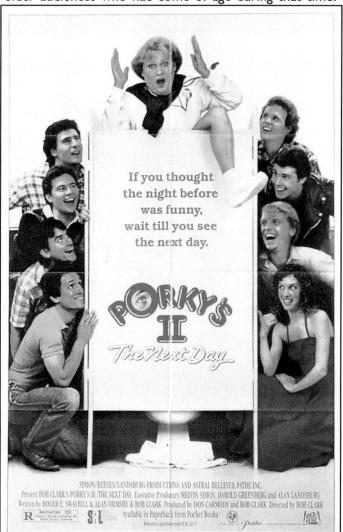

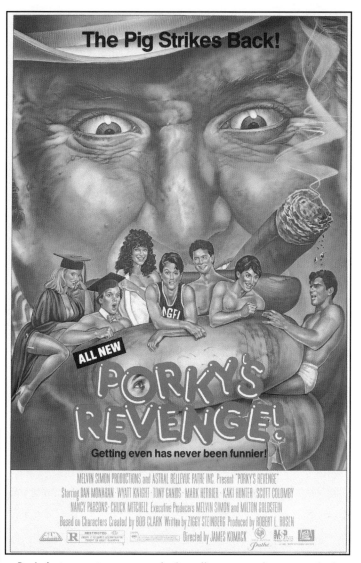

Porky's is set just as rock & roll was ready to explode, so country blues and doo-wop are still popular with the teens, and the film's soundtrack is packed with choice cuts from legends like Hank Williams, Patti Page, The Platters and Les Paul.

Despite its crude nature, *Porky's* does have an endearing, cheeky charm, and its own sense of innocence. In light of its box-office success, a sequel was no surprise, and *Porky's II: The Next Day* (1983) soon followed. Despite the return of Bob Clark and most of the original cast (one notable absence being Porky himself), *Porky's II: The Next Day* failed to capture the spark which made the first film gel so well with audiences. Despite the sequel earning only a third of what *Porky's* did, it was still successful enough to warrant a third and final film, *Porky's Revenge* (1985). Porky was back, but Bob Clark was gone, and the downhill slide for the series continued, though some considered it a mild improvement on its predecessor, and it also benefited from an excellent, bluesy rock & roll soundtrack produced by Dave Edmunds and featuring the likes of Jeff Beck, George Harrison, Carl Perkins, and The Fabulous Thunderbirds.*

"See it or be it..."

Arriving in American cinemas a few months after *Porky's*, *The Last American Virgin* (1982) had an interesting history to it. Produced by the infamous Cannon Films, headed by the team of Menahem Golan and Yoram Globus, it was essentially an Americanized remake of Israeli director Boaz Davidson's own *Eskimo Limon* (1978, AKA *Lemon Popsicle*). *Eskimo Limon* became the highest-grossing film in Israeli history, and spawned several sequels, so when Golan and Globus took over Cannon in the late '70s, it seemed a natural idea to bring Davidson to America to direct films for them.

Like *Porky's*, *Eskimo Limon* was set in the '50s and was based on Davidson's own experiences growing up in Israel during that time. For *The Last American Virgin*, which Davidson also wrote along with directing, the story was kept firmly in the pulsing day-glow of 1982 and powered along by a soundtrack filled with new wave pop-rock numbers by The Police, Devo, The Cars, Blondie and even the young U2! Other than updating the time and location, the film could have been made straight from a translated screenplay of its Israeli big brother to the point that even a few Israeli customs and mannerisms are worked into it, giving it a bit of a quirky tone at times (it must be a common practice in Israel to bring a large bag of oranges as a gift to someone in hospital?!?).

The plot of *The Last American Virgin* once again centers on a group of horny high school males desperate to start sowing their wild oats. Gary (Lawrence Monoson) works as a pizza delivery driver after school, and never enjoys the same level of success with girls as his two best friends, the smooth and slick Rick (Steven Anion), and the chubby but confident David (Joe Rubbo). When Gary falls for super-cute new student Karen (Diane Franklin), he is devastated to find out that she is instead interested in Rick, who only wants to use Karen for sex. Like *Porky's*, *The Last American Virgin* does have its darker undertones, when Karen falls pregnant to Rick, who quickly rejects her, and the ending doesn't bring the happiness for the lead character that it usually would in this type of film.

The Last American Virgin was an early starring role for Diane Franklin, who I developed an unashamed crush

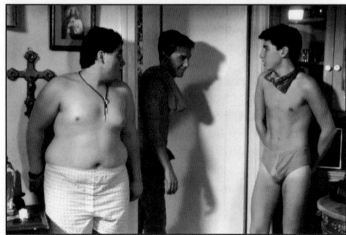

on in the mid '80s. Nothing too remarkable or unique about a young film-lover harbouring a bit of a thing for an unattainable celebrity, the curious exception here being that I fell for Franklin three times in different movies before I realised I was smitten by the same actress, so effective was her ability to completely disappear, chameleon-like, into her roles (no matter how lightweight those roles may have seemed on paper). In *Amityville II: The Possession* (1982) she portrayed the teenaged Patricia, innocent and sweet yet aroused by dark, forbidden sexuality. In 'Savage' Steve Holland's brilliant teen romance comedy *Better Off Dead* (1985) she was the petite and intelligent French exchange student living next door to dumped, depressed everyman John Cusack, while in the live-action comic book horror of *TerrorVision* (1986) she was the exaggerated Cyndi Lauper-esque valley girl trying to deal with a dysfunctional family and a blob from outer space that was slowly devouring the whole household. While the mainstream media may have been touting Molly Ringwald as the queen of '80s teen cinema, for me that tiara always belonged to Diane Franklin. Apart from always being so much fun to watch, I think I identified with (and was attracted to) the 'misfit' side that inhabited so many of her characters.

"They're getting a little behind in their homework."
Putting an established teen idol in a teen sex comedy was a guaranteed way to get some press and increase the chance of the film finding an audience, and in 1982 there were few bigger teen idols than Scott Baio. Gaining fame as a child actor playing Chachi Arcola, the young cousin of Fonzie (Henry Winkler) in *Happy Days* and its spin-off, *Joanie Loves Chachi*, Baio had also appeared in the movies *Bugsy Malone* (1976), *Skatetown U.S.A.* (1979) and *Foxes* (1980), and by the early '80s he was being prominently featured on the cover of just about every issue of teen magazines like '16' and 'Tiger Beat'. So when Baio was cast as the lead in *Zapped!*, it received quite a bit of coverage in the teen publications, who usually shied away from teen sex comedies due to their nudity and more sleazy nature.

Accurately described by more than one critic as being like a bad Disney movie with added nudity, *Zapped!* aims to be a teen sex riff on telekinesis horror films like *Carrie* (1976) and *The Spell* (1977). Baio plays bookish science student Barney Springboro, who develops the ability to move objects with his mind after an accident occurs during his experiments in the science lab. While he initially uses his newfound powers for his own harmless amusement, causing doors to slam shut, posters to fall off classroom walls, and helping the local baseball team hit a home run, Barney is eventually persuaded by his best friend Peyton Nichols (Willie Aames) to put his gift to more salacious uses, particularly when it comes to stripping the clothes off blonde Jane Mitchell (Heather Thomas), a beautiful but very vain and stuck-up student in their class. As in *Carrie*, the film climaxes with the high

SCOTT BAIO and WILLIE AAMES

*The comedy
that won't
let you down.*

Zapped!

They're
getting a
little behind
in their
classwork.

school prom, but instead of blood and carnage, Barney sends a wild gust of wind through the auditorium, tearing away everybody's clothes and sending them running off in embarrassment.

A ludicrous film on every level, *Zapped!* at least has an attractive cast to keep things interesting during its frequent dull spots. Like Baio, curly-haired Willie Aames was also something of a late '70s teen idol, having appeared as Tommy Bradford in the dramedy series *Eight is Enough*. Baio and Aames had enough screen chemistry that they were later cast together for the long-running sitcom *Charles in Charge*. The great Scatman Crothers turns up as the baseball coach, notorious (and troubled) screen geek Eddie Deezen puts in an appearance, and Heather Thomas, then one of television's 'It' girls thanks to her role on *The Fall Guy*, is inarguably a stunning screen beauty. *Zapped!* was Thomas' first feature film, and it turned out to be controversial for her, with the actress unhappy that a body double was brought in to provide nude inserts for her character. Thomas also filed a complaint when the film included a shot of a photo that appeared to depict her face photoshopped onto a naked body. The minor controversy, and the coverage it received on showbiz news reports like *Entertainment Tonight*, helped give *Zapped!* a little extra zap at the box-office, and its subsequent life on home video led to a belated sequel, *Zapped Again* (1990), which featured none of the original film's central cast, but at least had Linda Blair and Karen Black. As an interesting piece of film trivia for horror fans, *Zapped!* was photographed by the cinematographer of *The Texas Chain Saw Massacre* (1974), Daniel Pearl.

"The last word about the first time."

When it comes to future superstars who landed an early role in a teen sex comedy, there would likely be none bigger than Tom Cruise, who found himself top-billed in Curtis Hanson's *Losin' It* (1983). 1983 was a breakout year for Cruise, starting with a supporting role in Francis Ford Coppola's *The Outsiders* and following-up *Losin' It* with lead roles in the teen comedy drama *Risky Business* and the sports drama *All the Right Moves*. Quality wise, *Losin' It* may seem like the dud in that four-pack, but Hanson knew how to put together a strong and entertaining movie, as he would later prove with hits like *The Hand that Rocks the Cradle* (1992), *L.A. Confidential* (1997) and *8 Mile* (2002). *Losin' It* is certainly not on the same level as those later films, but for the genre it is working within it can hold its head up high, and remains a fun watch.

Another period piece, *Losin' It* is set in mid '60s Los Angeles, and follows the adventures of three high school buddies who take a road trip to Tijuana, Mexico, planning to lose their virginity to one of the local hookers at a bargain price (Tijuana, of course, is known as a spot where every price is usually up for bargaining). Tagging along with Woody (Cruise), Dave (Jackie Earl Haley) and Spider (John Stockwell) is Dave's younger brother, Wendell (John P. Navin, Jr.), who is more interested in obtaining illegal fireworks than he is in picking up girls. En route to the border they pick up Kathy (Shelly Long), a young lady hitching her way to Mexico to file for a quickie divorce. Predictably, when the group finally hit Tijuana, the four

"The last word...about the first time."

A JOEL B. MICHAELS-GARTH H. DRABINSKY PRODUCTION · LOSIN' IT ·
starring TOM CRUISE, JACKIE EARLE HALEY, JOHN STOCKWELL and SHELLEY LONG
original music by KEN WANNBERG written by B.W.L. NORTON · B.W.L. NORTON · BRYAN GINDOFF
produced by BRYAN GINDOFF and HANNAH HEMPSTEAD
executive producers JOEL B. MICHAELS and GARTH H. DRABINSKY directed by CURTIS HANSON

boys are totally ill-prepared for the reality of life, getting conned by experienced street ladies, buying aspirin in the belief it is Spanish fly, and running afoul of enraged and aggressive older brothers of the local girls. Woody also finds himself becoming attracted to the older Kathy, and she responds to his sweet and gentle side, sharing a night of tenderness and passion before she ultimately decides to return to her husband.

While Cruise's charisma and all-American charm are clearly prominent in *Losin' It*, the other performances and characterizations are just as important to the film, especially those from Shelley Long, with her impeccable comic timing, the distinctive and always-excellent Jackie Earl Haley, and John P. Navin, Jr. as the nerdy, entrepreneurial young Wendell (nicknamed "Wimp"). Cruise may have been a superstar in waiting, but *Losin' It* performed poorly at the box-office and was savaged by most critics, though it found a new life and a much bigger audience on home video.

"More fun than games!"

Video games and video arcades were an integral part of many teenagers' lives during the '80s, particularly in America. The local games arcade, usually situated inside a sprawling suburban shopping mall, became a popular spot to meet up with friends and sweethearts, and generally mingle and be seen while feeding quarter after quarter into the latest game.

Directed by Greydon Clark, an exploitation filmmaker with such credits to his name as *Black Shampoo* (1976), *Satan's Cheerleaders* (1977) and *Without Warning* (1980), *Joysticks* (1983) casts the great Joe Don Baker as a shady businessman who, with the help of his two inept nephews, plots to shut down the local video arcade, which is where all the hot gals hang out and divert the boys' attention from their games. Clark came up with the idea for the film while attending a Texas test screening of his previous film *Wacko* (1982) and noticed all the teenagers and kids who were lining up to play the video games in the cinema's lobby. The original title for the film was *Video Madness*, before Clark decided on the more memorable, and innuendo-filled *Joysticks*.

JOY STICKS
A Greydon Clark Production
Starring Joe Don Baker, Leif Green, Jim Greenleaf, Scott McGinnis
Director of photography Nicholas Von Sternberg
Written by Al Gomez & Mickey Epps and Curtis Burch
Produced and directed by Greydon Clark

Filled with footage of all the classic arcade games of the day in action (particularly during the climactic video game showdown), *Joysticks* also contains what is probably the best original theme song to a teen sex comedy from this era. Performed by an obscure band called Legion, the new wave-tinged pop rock track is played over the opening credits, as a sexy blonde in short shorts bounces about in front of an arcade game, and features classic lyrics like:

> *Wiggle left, jerk it right*
> *Shoot fast, shoot straight*
> *Playing with my joystick!*

In 2016, Eczema Records in the US released the soundtrack to *Joysticks* for the first time, in a limited pressing of 800 copies on pink vinyl and 200 copies on red vinyl, which included an old-school dot matrix fanzine featuring new interviews with several of the cast and crew members.

"The nuts who always score!"

While technically a Canadian production (it was filmed in and around the Ontario area), I'm including *Screwballs* here because it follows the teen sex comedy template so faithfully, and has always been one of my personal favourites, mainly because of how unashamedly silly it is,

and because of some of the interesting names involved. Set in the mid '60s (though a pinball machine for '70s glam rock group KISS is visible in one scene), *Screwballs* has five boys from T & A High School meeting up in detention and planning revenge on the person they blame for sending them there, the virginal Purity Busch (Linda Speciale). As you can see, *Screwballs* does not rely on subtlety to get its points across, even when compared to its contemporaries (other character names include Goodhead, Jerkovski, Boudoir, and Principal Stuckoff!). The highlight of all the lunacy is undoubtably the impromptu game of strip bowling that breaks out between the boys and girls at the local alley, which end with the bespectacled geeky kid getting a bowling ball stuck to his privates, relief only coming when the girls tease him to orgasm, sending the ball flying off down the lane for a full strike!

Screwballs was popular enough to warrant two sequels, *Loose Screws* (1985) and *Screwball Hotel* (1988). Director Rafal Zielinski also helmed two other sex comedies - the *Police Academy* riff *Recruits* (1986) and *State Park* (1988), which is best known for its poster art depicting a randy grizzly bear chasing a bikini-clad blonde. The following decade, he stunned and surprised many people (including myself) with the dark, grungy crime drama *Fun* (1994) starring Alicia Witt and Renee Humphrey and based on the true story of two teenaged girls who murdered an elderly lady in California in 1983, claiming they did it "just for fun". A film which came out

of left field when considering Zelinski's previous work, *Fun* is a stark and disturbing tale that deserves to be more widely known than it currently is. In a curious way, it makes the director's teen sex comedy films seem a lot more fascinating in retrospect, knowing the capabilities of the mind behind them. It's also interesting to note that the screenplay for *Screwballs* was co-written by star Linda Shayne (who plays bubbly blonde Bootsie Goodhead), in collaboration with Jim Wynorski, the prolific writer/director of numerous low-budget exploitation films, many of which went straight-to-video in the '80s and '90s.

The scene in *Screwballs* that takes place at a drive-in was filmed at the old TePee Drive-In in Pickering, Ontario, which operated between 1963-1991, and was unique in that it was a combined indoor/outdoor venue, with space for 300 cars under the roof and another 100 outside.

"Iowa's #1 nerd takes revenge!"

The American spring break, which usually occurs around March/April each year, has long been a fabled period where American college students flock to sunny climes to cut loose, party down, chase girls and dry out behind the ears. It provided the perfect set-up for a teen sex comedy, and one of the best was *Fraternity Vacation* (1985), directed by James Frawley, who was mostly known as a prolific director of episodic television shows like *The Monkees*, *Colombo*, *Magnum, P.I.*, *Law & Order* and many others.

Fraternity Vacation provided an early role for future Hollywood heavyweight Tim Robbins, playing Harry 'Mother' Tucker, a senior from Iowa State's Theta Pi Gamma fraternity, who heads to Palm Springs for spring break with his best friend Joe Gillespie (Cameron Dye). As frequently happens in these movies, the pair are saddled with a nerdy youngster, this time in the form of potential pledge Wendall Tvedt (Stephen Geoffreys), whose father has offered the use of his Palm Springs condo if Harry and Joe can

help his son find a girl and become a bit more worldly. When the group encounter some guys from a rival fraternity, they make a bet as to who can score first with beautiful, classy co-ed Ashley Taylor (Sheree J. Wilson). The usual sexual (and sexist) hijinks ensue, including a romp with Barbara Crampton and Kathleen Kinmont, two actresses who played the female leads in *Re-Animator* (1985) and *Bride of Re-Animator* (1990) respectively.

Crampton's presence certainly helps increase the appeal of *Fraternity Vacation* for cult film fans, and it's fun seeing Robbins in this kind of role, but the acting honours here easily belong to Stephen Geoffreys, who later the same year would appear in his best-known role, playing 'Evil Ed' in Tom Holland's *Fright Night* (1985). Later, Geoffreys reportedly appeared in gay porn films under the name Sam Ritter. The interesting cast of *Fraternity Vacation* is rounded out by Britt Ekland and John Vernon, while TV sit-com fans will enjoy seeing Max Wright from *Alf* and Amanda Bearse from *Married with Children* in supporting roles. It would be one of the last decent entries in that initial post-*Porky's* wave of teen sex comedies.

Also Recommended:

My Tutor (1983), *The First Turn-On!* (1983), *Spring Break* (1983), *Up the Creek* (1984), *Hot Moves* (1984), *Hot Dog... The Movie* (1984), *Hardbodies* (1985), *Mischief* (1985).

Further Recommended Reading:

'The Excellent Adventures of the Last American, French-Exchange Babe of the '80s' by Diane Franklin
(2012/Self-Published)

In 'The Excellent Adventures of the Last American, French-Exchange Babe of the '80s', Diane Franklin looks back on her childhood in Plainview, Long Island, her teen modelling career and early appearances on daytime soaps and TV movies of the week, and of course the '80s films for which she is so fondly remembered. Apart from the films already mentioned, Franklin also appeared in *Second Time Lucky* (1985) and *Bill & Ted's Excellent Adventure* (1989). Each film is given a brief chapter, and in a fun little touch Diane gives each chapter a film-like 'rating' that warns younger readers about any upcoming racy material!

This isn't some tell-all, scandalous cash grab, nor is it an in-depth autobiography of Diane Franklin's private life. It's more like the ultimate souvenir scrapbook of her career, presented in a way that allows Franklin's infectious personality to shine through. She just seems like such a genuinely nice, positive, and upbeat person, happy with where she is in life and with an appreciative grasp on her contribution to '80s pop cinema culture. Breezy but entertaining, and filled with a wealth of terrific black & white photographs from all periods of Franklin's life and career. Available from Amazon.

'Teen Movie Hell' by Mike 'McBeardo' McPadden
(2019/Bazillion Points)

Subtitled "A crucible of coming-of-age comedies from *Animal House* to *Zapped!*", 'Teen Movie Hell' is an indispensable volume for any fan of the genre. Written with his usual wit and style by the late Mike McPadden (who sadly died suddenly not long after the book's publication), 'Teen Movie Hell' celebrates its subject joyously, and comes heavily illustrated in black & white and an eight-page colour section. If video stores were still around, 'Teen Movie Hell' would have been the essential tome to have with you as you wade through the weekly rental shelves in the comedy aisle.

*In 2009, noted Australian exploitation filmmaker Brian Trenchard-Smith directed *Porky's Pimpin' Pee Wee*, a low-budget quickie that briefly screened online but has never been officially released, and was produced only so the companies involved, Mola Entertainment and Lontano Investments, could retain the rights to the *Porky's* name and franchise.

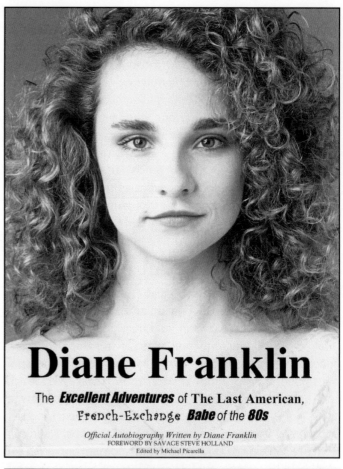

Diane Franklin
The *Excellent Adventures* of The Last American, French-Exchange *Babe* of the *80s*
Official Autobiography Written by Diane Franklin
FOREWORD BY SAVAGE STEVE HOLLAND
Edited by Michael Picarella

TEEN MOVIE HELL
A CRUCIBLE OF COMING-OF-AGE COMEDIES FROM ANIMAL HOUSE TO ZAPPED!
MIKE "McBEARDO" McPADDEN

TOUGH GUYS DON'T DANCE

by Aaron Stielstra

"He didn't care about accuracy, and he didn't care about people being confused. It was like he was going to make his imprint, and…whatever." - D.A. Pennebaker, documentarian and cinematographer for Norman Mailer.

A truly botched masterpiece - about what, and for whom, it's hard to grasp - rarely has a movie blown minds (or just disappointed them) like *Tough Guys Don't Dance* (1987). No other modern noir, let alone a straight movie, contains the kind of blowhard excesses that writer-director Norman Mailer pioneered in his earlier cinema experiments. Yet, at the same time, the author's 'you-guys-just-film-it-and-we'll-do-it' dogma gives way to a hard-boiled narrative. It packs the complex storyline and characters of a noir while drenching the viewer in unique 'Maileresque' pulp.

The pulp kings at Cannon Films produced a number of commendable yet wobbly prestige movies in the '80s like John Cassavetes' *Love Streams* (1984), Robert Altman's *Fool for Love* (1985) and Barbet Schroeder's *Barfly* (1987), as well as films by Andrei Konchalovsky, Peter Bogdanovich and Franco Zeffirelli. Mailer got his chance too, and revived his irregular film expression within a well-paced narrative. But behind all the elements of the genre (two-timing women, memory loss, gruesome murders) there is concealed a whole lot more - mostly madness.

Thankfully, *Tough Guys Don't Dance* doesn't work like a premeditated cult movie, which earns it some street cred and a warped charm. Even during its more exaggerated moments, director Mailer seems to be presenting nothing less than legitimate drama, even tragedy. Furthermore, it can't be labelled a failed attempt at a David Lynch-style noir, which it echoes in places (frequent Lynch composer Angelo Badalamenti even provides the lush score), or Alan Rudolph's *Trouble in Mind* (1985). With a defiant, profane and booze-soaked intellectual's approach to the genre, the film rejects all sophisticated touches and embraces its own signature chaos.

Mailer himself described the film as a "subtle horror movie", though to be honest subtlety is missing completely. To think of it as anything other than a Normal Mailer movie is to miss out on a wild, abnormal experience, despite the melodic music and catchy title. Very little normality follows the opening credits.

In place of the quasi-journalism and aimless plotlines contained in early Mailer movies like *Wild 90* (1968) and *Beyond the Law* (1968), there *is* a discernible story. Unlike in *Maidstone* (1970), if you desire some kind of plot, you don't have to consult Wikipedia.

81

It revolves around alcoholic writer Tim Madden (Ryan O'Neal) awakening from a 5-day binge. Instead of finding a dented car in his driveway or puddles of vomit on the stairs, he's launched into a forced recollection of events that involve blood, bourbon and severed blonde heads.

The story is compelling and O'Neal really sells his murky role, looking puffy and deflated, yet somehow still handsome, as he tries to remember how he ended up in this sticky situation.

Flashbacks give us some pieces of the puzzle. More interesting, the movie packs enough turgid, inspired characterizations into its two hours to rival the fevered storytelling of Jim Thompson. Who needs a linear plot when there are so many weirdos popping up everywhere?

Additionally, there are also some of the best coke-sniffing '80s party extras to appear on film, rampant vulgarity, homophobia, seances, drug deals, mysterious tattoos, triple-X rated actresses turned Santa Barbara realtors, Christian swingers, gangs of hot-rod thugs, some truly godawful southern accents and enough vicious blonde females - later, corpses - to frighten Sam Peckinpah. Clarence Williams III cameos as 'Bolo'. It says much that Lawrence Tierney, as O'Neal's dad, ends up being the most normal member of the cast!

While Madden tries to unravel the mystery of his past five days, one memory-nightmare leads to another. Most of these flashbacks reveal his sordid marriages and Madden's inability to avoid keeping the most destructive company.

As always, Mailer's directorial mistakes (or the decisions most other directors wouldn't make) translate into his own film grammar. It's a style which leads to some memorable acting.

Miserable O'Neal, surrounded by perverts and fiends, comes across as a trapped but not very tainted character. Unlike other noir protagonists, he seems like he belongs in this world - not so much unsurprised by the mayhem as only mildly corrupted.

O'Neal's now infamous "Oh God, oh man!" soliloquy on the beach is a perfect example of Mailer attempting some kind of theatrical expressionism to broadcast Madden's desperation. Others would just call it really bad direction and acting.

O'Neal, himself, took Mailer to task for the indulgence, and it harkens back to Rip Torn attacking Mailer on camera with a hammer in *Maidstone*, the actor exercising berserk improvisation in response to what he considered incompetent leadership. According to Torn, he was sleepless yet 'wired' at the time.

Since Mailer's early films bludgeoned their small audiences with a mixture of sloppy documentary tactics, noise and bad acting (to witness Mailer himself playing a gangster in *Beyond the Law* makes for excruciating viewing), here it's a relief to see the movie features good actors, even if they struggle at times to maintain their balance or protect

their careers.

Deborah Sandlund plays Madden's ex-wife Patty Lareine, the most grotesque of the women in the story, a misogynist creation so absurd and offensive that she seems to have stepped out of an old, poor-man's Mickey Spillane short story in a 'True Detective' porno mag. Her shrill performance is a challenge for viewers more comfortable with the less-is-more school of acting, or maybe just anyone who generally prefers the Sally Field style. Sandlund's South Carolina accent alternates between Yosemite Sam and a birdcall.

The other women in the film are given either oblivious, weak natures or suffer savage, nymphomaniac hysteria. Many survive Mailer's universe with their talents intact. Frances Fisher, as the porn-star turned realtor Jessica Pond, boasts an incredible laugh. Isabella Rossellini plays O'Neal's ex-wife, Madeleine, and, as she did in *Blue Velvet* (1986), endures abuse with some dignity while burdened with an unflattering page-boy haircut.

Not to be outdone, Wings Hauser appears as Vietnam-vet police-chief psychopath Alvin Luther Regency, who invades O'Neal's paranoid, drunken-stupor world. Mailer seems to be resurrecting this nightmare creation from his earlier novels concerning machismo, like 'Why Are We in Vietnam?'. You wonder if he saw Gary Sherman's thriller *Vice Squad* (1982) and decided to allow Hauser more screen-time to perform his unhinged schtick as

Ramrod the killer pimp. In every snake-eyed, lip-smacking monologue, Hauser wins hands-down in the 'disturbing actor' sweepstakes. In a movie densely populated with scenery-chewers, that's no mean feat.

Lawrence Tierney provides the entertaining black comedy moments, and the movie needs every single one of them. Tierney's raspy voice of reason is not only surprising, it's like a classic noir presence from the past suddenly joining Mailer's lunatic party of modern noir grotesques. Without any Bruce Willis smirking, he mutters: "I say we deep-six the heads. You got an anchor?" And it seems a perfectly reasonable solution.

Mailer's setting - the normally hip artist colony of Provincetown, Massachusetts - is transformed into a location as berserk as its residents, becoming some kind of depraved Cabot's Cove from *Murder, She Wrote*. But if Angela Lansbury were on hand to witness this kind of murderous mess (forget solving it), she'd likely drop the case.

Norman Mailer's dialogue wanders in and out of reality, as well. It's hard to decide if the Pulitzer Prize-winning writer-director's lines like "I'm no more of a slut than any faggot!", or, my favourite: "That shit was too heavy to

flush!" are there only to give characters colorful outbursts. Or, they serve to replace the usual cryptic exposition found in noirs. Or maybe it's just more fun to supply a noir with lines like "Certain dames ought to wear a T-shirt that say, 'Hang around, I'll make a cocksucker out of you'."

Even more dumbfounding is this exchange:

Capt. Alvin Luther Regency: I made you come 16 times... in a night.

Madeleine: Not one of them was good.

Capt. Alvin Luther Regency: That's because... ya got no WOOOOOMB!

It's almost as if Samuel Fuller and Paul Morrissey collaborated.

The movie flew above and below audience radars. It mostly collided with them, briefly, and struck most as horrific, desperate and wrong. Despite excellent production values and beautiful photography by John Bailey, it's a movie at war with itself. No amount of aesthetic design can compete with its audacity, and its eccentric moments are there to be remembered. Mailer's fraudulent reality has never been more extreme than when it's trapped in a straight story.

How do you present a noir story with melodramatic orchestration, then pump a Pam Tillis pop song entitled *Real Man* over the credits like we just watched a dance movie with Kevin Bacon?

The prestigious Actor's Studio is thanked in the

credits. But after watching so many blustery, shrieking performances in one movie, it's hard not to think crabby despot Lee Strasberg was disappointed.

Even poor Francis Ford Coppola's Zoetrope Studios, who co-produced, must have been dismayed at the unsavoury failure Mailer's film turned out to be. This, after a long series of boring yet savoury failures.

Mailer's oddball entry did fail at the box office, but its reviews were hardly run of the mill dismissals. Reactions often traded "terrible" for "wonderful" within the same review, and they are almost as entertaining as the movie, itself, which further earned 7 nominations in the Golden Raspberry Awards.

Mailer accepted his Golden Raspberry for worst director, but he likely accepted the award because it was another spotlight and he loved all the spotlights he could find. As 'Washington Post' critic Hal Hinson pointed out: "it's a film that supplies homosexual panic as well as something you can watch in stunned amazement. Watching Mailer direct *Tough Guys Don' Dance* is like watching a guy climb behind the wheel of a powerful sports car and slam it, full speed, into the wall - then back up and slam into it again. And there's a fascination in seeing this kind of spectacle because it's not just anybody behind the wheel - it's Norman Mailer."

If people could stomach (or enjoy) the obnoxious speechifying and nonsense in *Maidstone*, at least here the love/hate relationship toward audience expectations is on par with the rebellious shock value found in John Waters. At about the film's midpoint ("Oh God, oh man!"), it becomes very obvious Mailer is definitely now behind the wheel.

Tough Guys Don't Dance might wear an outlaw/cult film badge, but there's no membership to that club. It sticks to the director's cockeyed vision even as it's going over the waterfall. At least you can enjoy its absurdity and bad taste while watching a *Twin Peaks* fan flee the movie because of these same qualities.

Cannon was as commercially minded as any other studio, though, more often than not, lost, blind, stumbling and full of toxic hubris. It's still sad to hear people think *Tough Guys Don't Dance* is the worst film Cannon produced. (did these folks never see *Over the Top*

[1987] or *Outlaw of Gor* [1989]?)

Cannon didn't interfere with Tobe Hooper's *Texas Chainsaw Massacre 2* (1986) or alter its course, even allowing it an X-rating. This was how I saw the movie at a memorable Tucson, Arizona drive-in screening. By the end of it, there were only two cars remaining, one of which was a trailer the drunken theater caretaker lived in while chasing kids away when thy tried to climb the perimeter fence. It's obvious that Cannon responded in similar fashion to Norman Mailer and his imprint as it progressed from widespread to epidemic levels. It's unthinkable any studio would allow a filmmaker that kind of freedom nowadays.

If John Wayne's famous advice about frontier survival - "never apologize, it's a sign of weakness" - applied to the world of Mailer's film, then one of the lines spoken by Patty Lareine would say it best: "Pardon my French, motherfucker!"

85

THE THREE GREAT SCI-FI REMAKES OF THE '80s

by James Aaron

Ah, the movie remake. That reviled and ridiculed phenomenon. Up go the cries of "Isn't there an original idea left in Hollywood?" as we're subjected to a deluge of *A Star is Born*s, *Ocean's Eleven*s, *True Grit*s, and *The Wicker Man*s (sheesh, what were they thinking with *that* one?), not to mention the endless parade of superhero movies and Bond adventures. Science fiction and horror seem particularly rife with remake fever, especially after a decade-long run of revamps kicked off with Marcus Nispel's *The Texas Chainsaw Massacre* (2003) and trampled across the sacred territory of virtually any horror classic from the '70s and '80s worth mentioning… and more than a few not worth mentioning.

Frequently spat upon by artists, audiences and internet critics alike, remakes in general have long been a staple of Hollywood. Cecil B. DeMille made a silent *The Ten Commandments* in 1923, then directed the remake himself with color and sound in 1956. In fact, many silent films were remade once the 'talkie' became a standard movie experience - *Ben-Hur*, *The Thief of Bagdad*, *Nosferatu*, *The Cat and the Canary*, *The Mark of Zorro*, *The Wizard of Oz* and *The Phantom of the Opera* rank among the most famous examples. (For the purposes of this article, I am calling them remakes if they are new adaptations of the same literary source material, since that seems to be the running definition these days). And, if we're being honest, we can admit that a lot of these early do-overs actually did improve on their predecessors. Advances in filmmaking techniques allowed artists to better translate their creative vision to the silver screen. In the right artistic hands, innovation gave birth to a better brand of magic.

Since the dawn of the motion picture, science fiction and horror movies have proven time and again that they are uniquely ripe for rebirth via remake. These genres are more reliant on the best of contemporary technology to maximize the effectiveness of their story. Special effects and sound design in particular gain huge benefit from the giant leaps in capability that come with a couple of decades of advances.

These enhancements aren't just limited to computer processing power, either. Animatronics, makeup and prosthetics of today are all significantly improved from where they were in their heydays of the '80s and '90s, and as a result are more effective at selling fantasy now than ever before. We see increasing evidence of that as more directors turn to the on-set gratification of physical effects wherever possible, instead of sending every FX shot over to the computer lab, to be rendered in soulless pixels that will surely be considered low-res a few years later.

Yet even while we live through this renaissance in practical special effects, I'd like to whisk readers back to the glorious '80s where we can see three prominent examples of remakes outdistancing their prior versions. This trio staked out their territory at the nexus of horror and science fiction, as much a part of one genre as the other. Each sprang from a collaboration between visionary director and groundbreaking special effects artist, and might not have resulted in the same alchemy in anyone else's hands. Instead, they came together perfectly in just that special moment. As a result, these '80s films became classics in their own right. And they have only grown in stature since their original release: John Carpenter's *The Thing* (1982) and David Cronenberg's *The Fly* (1986) and Chuck Russell's *The Blob* (1988).

The Thing (1982)

Of these three greatest remakes, Carpenter's *The Thing* is almost surely the most beloved these days. Following an underwhelming initial box office performance, the movie finally gained its footing when it hit television and videocassette, and its stature has only grown over the ensuing decades. It's even taken another upward leap in the last ten years, when Carpenter has enjoyed renewed appreciation thanks to the popularity of Blu-ray and 4k special editions chock full of behind-the-scenes documentaries and glowing retrospectives.

Carpenter was already firmly established with both critics and audiences as a singularly talented filmmaker after a string of indie favorites in the '70s and early '80s - *Dark Star, Assault on Precinct 13, The Fog, Escape From New York* and the megahit *Halloween* - when he finally accepted Hollywood's overtures and agreed to take on *The Thing* for Universal. His remake of 1951's *The Thing from Another World* (directed by Christian Nyby) was meant as a more faithful adaptation of the original John W. Campbell story 'Who Goes There?'

Even then, Carpenter understood that any new take on the novella would be closely compared to the original Howard Hawks-produced movie. In fact, he'd long been a fan of that version, even referencing it onscreen during a scene in *Halloween* where a young boy watches the famous burn-in opening titles on television. (That reference came back around in glorious full circle when director David Gordon Green's *Halloween Ends* hit theaters in October 2022, and showed one of the more notable sequences from Carpenter's *The Thing* on a television set). In Carpenter's mind, the original was great on its own, and would be hard to surpass.

He needn't have worried.

It's true that the two stories share basic underpinnings. In both, a mismatched team of airmen and scientists find a spacecraft in the polar ice and are subsequently attacked by a strange alien lifeform that takes dogs as its earliest victims before moving on to the humans. Each of the films takes place in a harsh, isolated environment of ice and snow. But aside from that, things diverge quickly, and when they do, the '82 version proves superior at every turn.

First and foremost, the aliens themselves couldn't be more distinct. The threat in *The Thing from Another World*

The ultimate in alien terror.

JOHN CARPENTER'S
THE THING

A TURMAN-FOSTER COMPANY PRODUCTION JOHN CARPENTER'S 'THE THING'
KURT RUSSELL BILL LANCASTER ALBERT WHITLOCK ROB BOTTIN ENNIO MORRICONE DEAN CUNDEY LARRY FRANCO
WILBUR STARK STUART COHEN DAVID FOSTER & LAWRENCE TURMAN JOHN CARPENTER A UNIVERSAL PICTURE

is essentially a sentient plant, referred to in dialogue as both a "vegetable" and "an intellectual carrot." When it finally makes its first entrance, we get actor James Arness in a black flight suit, sporting spiky knuckles that make him look less carrot, more asparagus. Carpenter's creature, on the other hand - with full credit due to special effects wizard Rob Bottin - doesn't even *have* a specific form. Instead, the updated Thing is a shapeshifter that takes on the outer appearance of its host, while its own biology constantly evolves and assumes whichever characteristics of its victims it finds useful.

It's this shapeshifting that ingrains *The Thing* remake with its other defining trait: the deep paranoia that drives the story. In the Hawks-Nyby telling, the men and women of the polar station know their plant-based enemy and band together to fight it. It's a fairly straightforward man vs monster tale. In the Carpenter film, the all-male station crew don't have any idea *what* they're up against. As the alien picks them off one by one, they quickly realize that it's taking the form of its victims and that any one of them can be the monster at any time. That breaks down the group dynamic, making every man fend for himself and tightening the suspense in a way that *The Thing from Another World* never approaches.

Beyond the added suspense and origin of their titular aliens, perhaps the most cavernous advantage for the 1982 *The Thing* comes by way of its special visual effects, masterfully orchestrated by Bottin. There simply is no comparison between James Arness's asparagus knuckles and the slimy, sinewy, skin-ripping prosthetics that Bottin and Carpenter thrust upon the audience. Let's name just

a few: a head stretches and rips apart from its shoulders, a dog's face splits open like a time-lapse sunflower bloom; a man's chest caves in and becomes a toothy, forearm-eating mouth; a severed head sprouts spidery legs and scurries across the floor. To repeat an oft-quoted line from that scene: "You gotta be fuckin' kidding me!"

Not only are these spectacular visuals the biggest advantage of this remake, they're also responsible for its lasting impact on audiences even 40 years later. The 2011 version of *The Thing* (which was a prequel by name but honestly serves as more of a remake to the '82 movie than Carpenter's movie was to the Hawks-Nyby outing) generally eschewed physical effects for bland and mostly ineffective CGI, and paid the price with lackluster reviews and general audience apathy. Personally, this author thought that one was okay, but it certainly didn't sniff the same stratosphere of Carpenter's masterpiece.

Speaking of improved special effects...

The Fly (1986)

While *The Thing* set a remarkable standard for special effects in sci-fi horror and remains a powerful film that ranks among its director's best, for my money, the title of 'Best Remake of the '80s' belongs to David Cronenberg's *The Fly*. I'd even submit it as the best horror movie of the decade, the best science fiction movie of the decade and one of the five best movies of the decade, period.

In 1958, *The Fly* (directed by Kurt Neumann) told the schlocky story of a man who switches heads and a hand with a housefly, following a mishap with a molecular transporter. David Cronenberg - who in 1986 was already famous for his frequent examination of 'body horror' in films like *Videodrome, Rabid, Shivers* and *Scanners* - takes that nugget of an idea and explodes it. This is no simple sci-fi tale. Instead, Cronenberg seizes the opportunity and tells the emotionally complex story of a scientist, Seth Brundle (Jeff Goldblum), whose body undergoes an agonizing metamorphosis into an insect-like monster. Simultaneously, his mind also decays into that of an aggressive, trapped animal.

Such a graphic fantasy hinged on its special effects. If the metamorphosis wasn't believable, the story fell apart. Fortunately, FX artists Chris Walas and Stephen Dupuis delivered. Oh boy, did they deliver!

Cronenberg turned to Walas and Dupuis with confidence, after they had worked together on *Scanners*. Walas in particular was noted for his work on films like *Raiders of the Lost Ark, Enemy Mine* and most especially *Gremlins*. The pair's resulting work on *The Fly*, in terms of technical advances, was every bit as big a leap forward as *The Blob* and *The Thing* were from their earlier takes.

Where the '58 *The Fly* simply had actor David ('Al') Hedison don a fake hand and head, the 1986 team pulled together every trick at their disposal to portray

THE FLY

BE AFRAID.
BE VERY AFRAID.

BROOKSFILMS PRESENTS A DAVID CRONENBERG FILM THE FLY
JEFF GOLDBLUM GEENA DAVIS JOHN GETZ MUSIC BY HOWARD SHORE
SCREENPLAY BY CHARLES EDWARD POGUE AND DAVID CRONENBERG
PRODUCED BY STUART CORNFELD DIRECTED BY DAVID CRONENBERG

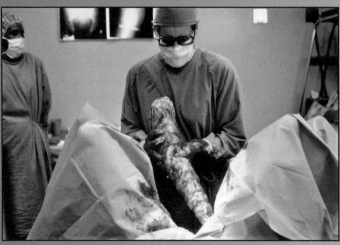

the disintegration of Goldblum's Seth Brundle, who transforms from man to Brundlefly following an accident during the testing of the teleportation pods he invented in his home laboratory. So groundbreaking was the stunning combination of makeup, prosthetics, puppeteering and animatronics that Walas and Dupuis took home a well-deserved Oscar for their work. (*The Thing* and *The Blob*, alas, were robbed in their respective years). It also won Walas the job as director of *The Fly II*, the-better-than-you-think 1989 sequel which, by design, is more straight-ahead monster movie while the Cronenberg picture ventured into murkier philosophical and ethical territory.

Yet for all its visual superiority and special effects mastery, it's the story's emotional resonance that places Cronenberg's *The Fly* far above the 1958 version. While the original *The Fly* carried traces of the DNA (sorry) that would come front and center in 1986 - the scientist is said to combine with the fly at an atomic level, and ultimately sacrifices himself before the fly takeover is complete - the technology at director Kurt Neumann's disposal was not nearly capable of taking the story to the visual and emotional depths reached by Cronenberg and company.

The heartbreaking tragedy that plays out between Goldblum's Seth Brundle and reporter Veronica Quaif (Geena Davis) has rarely been matched in horror and science fiction before or since. At first, she is attracted to his quirky but brilliant mind, only to see their love take a monstrous turn that ends with Brundle losing every shred of his outer humanity. Merged with both fly and machine, he lifts her shotgun to his head in one clawed hand, and the look in his insect eyes says it all as he silently begs Veronica to end his torment. Sobbing, she reluctantly pulls the trigger and grants his final wish. Then she throws the gun aside, and collapses on the laboratory floor in an emotionally spent heap.

The greatest movie monsters can pull from us jaded viewers that truest and rarest of human emotions - empathy. It's hard to imagine a similar impact involving a man in a suit jacket and a giant furry fly mask. To their everlasting credit, Cronenberg and Walas pulled it off to spectacular effect and gave us the greatest horror remake not just of the '80s, but of all time.

The Blob (1988)

Whenever the conversation turns to science fiction and horror movie remakes, *The Thing* and *The Fly* are always near the top of the list, if not Exhibit A and 1-A. But, surprisingly, the movie that bests the original version by the widest margin may actually be Chuck Russell's retelling of *The Blob*.

Perhaps this is owed to its director's relatively sparse ouvre. Chuck Russell's career only encompassed seven films from 1987-2016. Where Carpenter and Cronenberg are on the unquestioned Mt. Rushmore of horror directors list, some would take Russell's relatively small number of credits to mean he was a lesser director. Consider his first four pictures, though - the Freddy Kreuger vehicle *A Nightmare on Elm Street 3: Dream Warriors* (1987), *The Blob* (1988), *The Mask* (1994), a mega-success with Jim Carrey, and the Schwarzenegger action hit *Eraser* (1996). If you compare *The Blob* to those movies, it's fair to say the 1988 remake was one of the least financially successful films of Russell's career.

Yet, that doesn't take away from its artistic success, and its complete obliteration of the 1958 version, thanks to Russell's direction and the effects work of Tony Gardner.

Next to *The Thing from Another World* (1951) and *The Fly* (1958), *The Blob* circa 1958 (directed by Irvin S. Yeaworth, Jr.) isn't a particularly high bar to clear. The first *The Thing* had a moody atmosphere and effective polar setting to go with a mysterious story that kept things moving. *The Fly* had Vincent Price and... well, it had Vincent Price. *The Blob* didn't have much of anything worth noting, really. Outside of a stilted lead performance by a young Steve McQueen, the movie's biggest claim to fame is its opening credits song co-written by Burt Bacharach (!) which falsely promised the Blob "creeps, and leaps, and glides, and slides across the floor, right through the door, and all around the wall!" In reality, this Blob barely oozed and pulsated and looked for all the world like quivering jello during its brief

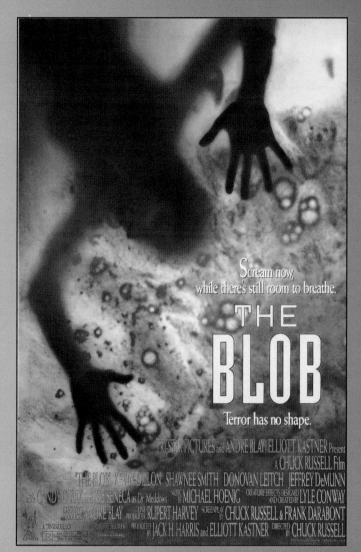

moments onscreen. Watching now, you can't help but wonder why folks didn't just sidestep the viscous bastard.

The 1988 edition of *The Blob* takes a completely different and infinitely more exciting tack. As with most remakes, some story aspects are the same - in both movies, the creature gets transported to the town hospital attached to the hand of a vagrant, then later attacks a movie theater and is ultimately defeated by cold chemicals - but for the most part, Russell gives his *The Blob* a new look and feel. If the original was a big yawn, the update is an eardrum-bursting scream in the middle of the night.

First, the 1988 movie never shies away from its monster. It's wall-to-wall Blob. It In the hands of Russell and special effects artist Tom Gardener - for whom the film was, unbelievably, his first major film credit - this monster is a real threat: fast, strong and *smart*. The horrific action strikes with a speed and shocking effectiveness that was completely impossible under the filmmaking limitations of the late '50s. Nobody could sidestep this one; it drops down on a victim from a hospital ceiling, crushes another inside a phone booth, pulls a poor man head-to-toe down a kitchen sink drain, and swallows up a child following a chase through the sewer. (Uh, spoiler alert.) It consumes teenagers and well-armed soldiers with equal aplomb.

This blob isn't just a shimmering wad of red goo, either; it shoots out icky pink tendrils and at times opens up a giant maw to welcome its unfortunate victims to their last moments.

In many ways, *The Blob* doesn't feel like a remake so much as a complete obliteration. The victims onscreen could be seen as stand-ins for Russell's own gleeful intentions - the director seemingly dead set on the complete and utter annihilation of the earlier *The Blob*. In a nonstop hail of thrills and top-notch special effects, he succeeds.

Perhaps Russell scared off the competition, too - his *The Blob* remains the only one of the three remakes discussed here not to since be remade or sequelized itself (yet).

Contemporary Cowboys of the '80s
LONE WOLF McQUADE and EXTREME PREJUDICE

El Paso is the 23rd largest city in America and one of the biggest in the southwestern United States. It's surprising more movies haven't been shot there, especially considering its striking vistas and its status as one of the safest cities in the country. True, *some* great films have been made there - Sam Peckinpah's *The Getaway* (1972), for example - but in the grand scheme of things there are surprisingly few. With its 81% Hispanic population and its position on the Rio Grande across from the highly populated Mexican city of Ciudad Juarez, you'd think El Paso would make an ideal backdrop for westerns in particular.

From the '80s - the decade of explosive, action-packed, meaty-fisted thrillers - I'd like to draw attention to two distinctive, fun and much-loved pictures set in El Paso which appeared within four years of each other. These 'modern westerns' (for want of a better phrase) are steeped in the cultural landscape of the era and feature top quality stars standing off, shooting out and slugging jaws. Cowboys and cowgirls, may I present for your enjoyment *Lone Wolf McQuade* (1983) and *Extreme Prejudice* (1987).

Directed by Steve Carver, *Lone Wolf McQuade* is one of karate-champion-turned-movie-star Chuck Norris' most fondly remembered vehicles. Interestingly, it was first intended as a project for top-bracket star Clint Eastwood. The Man from Malpaso turned it down, though you can easily envisage him in the title role, such is the balance of cop action, western tropes and the proliferation of Clint-isms which crop up throughout. The McQuade character is a man who likes to work alone, though he gets the

hump when his partner gets hurt (in this case, played by L.Q. Jones... the writing is immediately on the wall when he retires from the force in glory before agreeing to help out his old pal!) Then there is the clichéd, grumpy boss (R.G. Armstrong), who is great fun.

Carver had previously directed Norris in *An Eye for An Eye* (1981) so when Clint declined the part was soon offered to the celebrated martial artist. On the face of it, the script seemed to tie in perfectly with Chuck's ambition to grow his reputation as a chop-socky John-Wayne-for-the-masses. However, Norris wasn't initially keen on playing a character who drinks so much beer, as he wanted to be seen as a positive role model (amusingly, he had no problem whatsoever with viewers watching him kick the shit out of anyone who stands in his way). Funny as it might seem now, he also wasn't sure about growing a beard for the role. He eventually acquiesced and the beard, of course, is now seen as a key feature of Chuck's on-screen persona!

Anyone not convinced that the film aims to generate a modern-day Wild West vibe will immediately find their doubts dispelled by the opening credits, which play to the accompaniment of Francesco de Masi's pastiche spaghetti western title theme. The Rome-born composer had been providing music for westerns as far back as *The Shadow of Zorro* (1962), and could include *7 Dollars on Red* (1966), *Sartana's Here... Trade Your Pistol for a Coffin* (1970) and *Kid Vengeance* (1977) on his resumé. His evocative composition emphasises the genre feel created by shots of a wolf racing across the Texas plains. The connotations

could scarcely be stronger.

The post-credits scene sets its stall out by intercutting Norris - bearded, cowboy-hatted, sweat-drenched - using a modern rifle scope to spy on horse rustlers while police choppers soar above and the police department close in. There is a wonderful contrast between the slow, steady movements of McQuade the Texas Ranger and the frantic showdown far below between the Mexican rustlers and the regular cops. The showdown goes awry and the lawmen are brought to their knees - literally. McQuade rescues the situation by taking pot-shots from his high vantage point - scenes captured wonderfully by DoP Roger Shearman - before bringing the fight to ground level, shooting lots of people and generally blowing things up. This sequence foreshadows all that will follow: every action scene is a heightened Wild West movie trope, and all the more fun for it. The bad guy in this opening sequence is clearly inspired by classic spaghetti western villains, though the takedown with rapid-action automatic machine gun perhaps less so. Look out for a lovely shot of Norris silhouetted in long-shot, framed by the Texas sun - it's a timeless image!

The combination of traditional western and contemporary actioner is a tad cartoonish at times. At one point, R.G. Armstrong as the boss character gives McQuade a dressing down from behind his personal toilet door in his office. His grumpiness is pure caricature to the point of being silly. Yes, McQuade successfully busts criminal outfits, but what exactly does his boss want - for him to be nicer, cleaner and to go to church?!? We've seen variations on this disapproving authority figure many times but usually less ridiculous in presentation. Then there's the new Mexican partner Kayo (Robert Beltran), who is too hackneyed a creation, straight from the world of Clint's *Dirty Harry*. At least the role is well played.

Every western hero needs a worthy archenemy, and in this case David Carradine is perfectly cast. His wonderfully named Rawley Wilkes first appears around the quarter-hour mark, sucking a cigar and conducting an arms deal (they double-cross him, but he double-crosses them better with an added high kick!)

The introduction between McQuade and Wilkes is slightly contrived, especially as it manages to shoehorn in Barbara Carreras as a mutual love interest and Dana Kimmell as McQuade's daughter (and Wilkes' prospective hostage later in the story). However, it provides a good opportunity for some Carradine action in the competitive ring, followed by an old-fashioned saloon brawl in a more James Bondian setting of a flashy society party in exotic surroundings. Indeed, the low-key Bond similarities stretch to McQuade's rather silly supercharged jeep, and an even sillier later episode when he is buried in it underground, not to mention a villainous cackling dwarf who escapes a confrontation by using a revolving wall in his office! The

periodic B-movie Bond silliness doesn't quite fit, and one can't help thinking the makers would have been better remaining focused on the contemporary cowboy angle.

To be fair, the McQuade/Wilkes showdowns feel epic on a slightly lesser scale, with both actors exuding their own granite coolness. Norris' solidity contrasts well with Carradine's looseness. Chuck commented later: "David Carradine is every bit as good a martial artist as I am an actor." Take that as you will... but I suppose what Norris was trying to say was that their two styles meet effectively.

Critics correctly identified that the film adopts a pattern, repeated throughout, where 7 minutes of action are followed by 1 minute of talk. There's no denying the result is fast-paced fun. The fairly cringey romantic interlude is rather limp (montages of burgeoning love might best be left to westerns such as *Butch Cassidy and the Sundance Kid*) and the inevitability of L.Q. Jones getting offed and Robert Beltran suffering a bruising rite of passage are utterly obvious (why do these tough guys *ever* involve their old, trusted buddies or newbie partners... don't they know it's the kiss of doom every time?!) The addition of Federal interference and McQuade being placed on involuntary leave adds more (perhaps too much?) to the mix, but Carver knows how to shoot an action sequence and both Norris and Carradine know how to fill the screen with appealing testosterone.

Overall, Chuck's take on the persona of the heroic modern-day gunslinger is successful. He's perhaps not cut out for Clint's brand of hardboiled grit - thus, his estranged wife isn't actually estranged and his reaction to meeting his daughter's boyfriend is to pause... then smile and shake hands. However, as is always the case with movies like this, when he is pushed hard he comes back harder. And, boy, do the bad guys push him when they kill his pet wolf. I mean, yes, they *kidnapped* his daughter, but THEY *KILLED* HIS PET! Talk about a bad move! It all leads to a *High Noon*-style showdown - or *The Magnificent Seven* with reduced numbers if you like - and the climactic fight is genuinely engaging.

Lone Wolf McQuade saw Norris move from lower budget martial arts B-star to bona fide box office action star. And the beard stayed!

Four years later, the awesome director Walter Hill (of *Southern Comfort* and *48 Hours* fame) brought his own modern cowboys to El Paso in *Extreme Prejudice* (1987). For my money, this is a better film than *Lone Wolf McQuade*. As entertaining as the Norris entry is, Hill demonstrates a firmer understanding of what he is trying to do. Speaking afterwards, he said: "I don't think it was understood how much genre-parodying was involved in that picture." Well, maybe not by the critics, but it certainly seems obvious to me! The homages to Sam Peckinpah's *The Wild Bunch* (1969), the beautifully captured Texan hills and plains (courtesy of cinematographer Matthew F. Leonetti), the

ballsy music playing over a moody sunrise during the credits - the influences are plain to see. The score is provided by the always-reliable Jerry Goldsmith, with Ry Cooder credited as a 'source music producer'. The result is a truly authentic flavour.

More than anything, Hill's decision to cast Nick Nolte as Texas Ranger Jack Benteen and Powers Boothe as his criminal nemesis Cash Bailey ensures greatness. Hill explained: "I wanted someone who was representative of the tradition of the American West - taciturn, stoical, enduring. Someone who carried a lot of pain with him… I had him [Nolte] look at a lot of Gary Cooper films."

For his part, Nolte spent time tracking a real-life Ranger. He models his performance on him, right down to dialogue, mannerisms and dress. Boothe, Texan-born, makes the most of his villainous role, dressed all in white as a subversion of traditional western codes, but Nolte seems to have walked straight out of a page in history and into the 1980s. His introduction during a rainy night on the Texas/Mexican border offers a nice contrast to the typical dustbowl imagery (although there is plenty of that later). Western iconography proliferates - cowboy hats; the hero's long, all-weather duster coat with Sherriff's star; an antagonistic bar clientele; the slow, moody approach; bad guys sitting around a card table; casually held guns; handcuffs proffered; the bad guy being given the chance to "come in quietly" but rejecting it in favour of a doomed shootout. If it wasn't for the electric lighting and jukebox, the whole thing could be set in another century.

As Benteen's partner Hank Pearson (Rip Torn) says: "Just like ol' times."

The sharp, rugged, wise-cracking buddy act and an added fragile romance with Maria Conchita Alonso work well with the western framework but also point to the *Dirty Harry* era of contemporary cop thrillers. This is enhanced immeasurably by a sub-plot which does more than run below the surface. In fact, the movie opens with a lovely air of mystery as a series of ex-soldiers, presumed either missing or dead, are pictured arriving in Texas. This crew has the feel of a grown-up *A Team* and is blessed with a line-up including such strong actors as Michael Ironside, Clancy Brown and William Forsythe. They are involved in a clandestine military operation which involves conducting a bank heist (another familiar western trope).

In similar fashion (and not unlike *Lone Wolf McQuade*, superficially at least), genres blend throughout. For instance, take the scene where some drug dealers are brought to Cash by helicopter. Here we have modern machinery (a chopper) depositing the drug dealers (a modern replacement for old-school bandidos) and the principal antagonist toys with a scorpion in nerveless manner. We see him in close-up: stubbly, drenched in sweat, almost supernatural in his strong aura of menace. Goldsmith's score swirls around, sometimes referencing spaghetti western sounds, at other times conjuring ominous crime movie vibes. It all makes for a wonderful mix of sounds and styles.

Extreme Prejudice is loaded with gloriously quirky

characters and situations: the untrustworthy owner of a store, the bantering military misfits, etc. At one point, the gift of a white rabbit is revealed to be a bomb; at another, Mexican drug-runners stumble fatally into the pseudo-bank heist. The results are intoxicating.

The familiarity of the Old West pervades throughout. Benteen wants to meet Cash Bailey "at 12 noon" - of course he does! No other hour of the day has such significance within the genre. It's a great touch that Benteen and Bailey, adversaries on either side of the fence (literally and morally), are old friends. In *Lone Wolf McQuade*, relationships and events seem somewhat contrived, but that's not the case in *Extreme Prejudice*. Hill sets up a believable bunch of characters in a real world, and the script offers a plausible situation alongside characters of all shades and textures. There's a sense that they have been forced to share a lifetime in the same place, and we can tell there is context and background to the characters which extends well beyond the 105 minutes of the screenplay. As the Ranger points out, most criminals were once just "sweet kids." That's why Benteen and Bailey try to reason with each other; because they were childhood friends long ago. This kind of characterisation is nice to see. It adds depth. But at the end of the day, time has passed - one is now a Ranger, the other now a drug baron.

"You can't buy the badge," intones Nolte's character with classic reverence. To add to the stakes, his current squeeze is the villain's ex!

Now, if this had been a vintage western - say, early John Wayne or standard Audie Murphy - then the main storyline would've been enough, especially with Torn's buddy sheriff getting killed in a gunfight, creating angst and the need for payback. Here, though, the director manages to bring more to the table. Hill presents powerful, robust building blocks - that madcap *A Team* with added violence, the old friends either side of a border, all building up to a tense stand-off with bloody, brutal and explosive results.

Two members of the military - okay, let's call them the X Team - fake a fight to end up in jail for surveillance purposes. Meanwhile, divisions appear as Clancy Brown starts getting 'particular' about what he will and won't blow up, while Ironside claims the bank heist is "smoke and mirrors" (in reality, there is smoke within smoke and multiple mirrors). Hill muddies things, enabling these characters to be more than bad guys yet certainly not good guys. They wind up being tragic antiheroes in a final Peckinpah-style shootout.

The various threads pull together satisfyingly. Once one of the X Team dies and is revealed as apparently being already dead, it kicks off the next phase of the plot brilliantly, and the team's use of army terminology and principles allows a certain amount of sympathy for them, a necessity in order to permit the pathos of the finale.

The final third is almost a *Magnificent Seven* set-up as the

misunderstood antiheroes come together to sort things out, including their own mess. Throughout it all, the stoic Nolte character strides forth, ready to save the girl and do the right thing.

Lone Wolf McQuade and *Extreme Prejudice* offer a potent mix of action and thrills, both new-fangled and old-school in style. The latter wins this particular shootout by virtue of taking itself more seriously, but together they make for a fine double bill down in ol' El Paso.

Caricatures by Aaron Stielstra

Powers Boothe in *Extreme Prejudice* (pg. 93)

William Forsythe in *Extreme Prejudice* (pg. 93)

Kristy McNichol in *White Dog* (pg. 28)

Nick Nolte in *Extreme Prejudice* (pg. 93)

Tiny Lister and Luis Contreras in *Extreme Prejudice* (pg. 93)

CLOSING CREDITS

James Aaron

James is an American writer and film lover living in Kentucky with his wife and two dogs. He is the author (as Aaron Saylor) of three novels, including 'Sewerville' and 'Adventures in Terror', the latter of which is set during the horror movie and video store boom of the 1980s.

Rachel Bellwoar

Rachel is a writer for 'Comicon', 'Diabolique' magazine and 'Flickering Myth'. If she could have any director fim a biopic about her life it would be Aki Kaurismäki.

David Flack

David was born and bred in Cambridge. Relatively new to the writing game, he has had reviews published in 'We Belong Dead' and 'Cinema of the '70s'. He loves watching, talking, reading and writing about film and participating on film forums. The best film he has seen in over 55 years of watching is *Jaws* (1975). The worst is *The Creeping Terror* (1963) or anything by Andy Milligan.

John Harrison

John is a Melbourne, Australia-based freelance writer and film historian who has written for numerous genre publications, including 'Fatal Visions', 'Cult Movies', 'Is It Uncut?', 'Monster!' and 'Weng's Chop'. Harrison is also the author of the Headpress book 'Hip Pocket Sleaze: The Lurid World of Vintage Adult Paperbacks', has recorded audio commentaries for Kino Lorber, and composed the booklet essays for the Australian Blu-ray releases of *Thirst*, *Dead Kids* and *The Survivor*. 'Wildcat!', Harrison's book on the film and television career of former child evangelist Marjoe Gortner, was published by Bear Manor in 2020.

James Lecky

James is an actor, writer and occasional stand-up comedian who has had a lifelong obsession with cinema, beginning with his first visit to the Palace Cinema in Derry, (now long since gone) to see *Chitty Chitty Bang Bang* when he was six. Since then, he has happily wallowed in cinema of all kinds but has a particular fondness for Hammer movies, spaghetti westerns, Euro-crime and samurai films.

Simon J. Ballard

Simon lives in Oxford and works in its oldest building, a Saxon Tower. Whilst also working in the adjoining church, he has never felt tempted to re-enact scenes from *Taste the Blood of Dracula* or *Dracula A.D.1972*. He has never done this. Ever. He regularly contributes to the magazine 'We Belong Dead' and its various publications, and once read Edgar Allan Poe's 'The Black Cat' to a garden full of drunk young people at his local gay pub The Jolly Farmers. His first published work was a Top Tip in 'Viz' of which he is justifiably proud.

Jonathon Dabell

Jonathon was born in Nottingham in 1976. He is a huge film fan and considers '70s cinema his favourite decade. He has written for 'Cinema Retro' and 'We Belong Dead', and co-authored 'More Than a Psycho: The Complete Films of Anthony Perkins' and 'Ultimate Warrior: The Complete Films of Yul Brynner' with his wife. He lives in Yorkshire with his wife, three kids, three cats and two rabbits!

John H. Foote

John is a critic/film historian with thirty years experience. He has been a film critic on TV, radio, print criticism, newspaper and the web, for various sites including his own, Footeandfriendsonfilm.com. He spent ten years as Director of the Toronto Film School, where he taught Film History, and has written two books. The first was an exploration of the films directed by Clint Eastwood, the second a massive volume of the works of Steven Spielberg. Scorsese is next. John has interviewed everyone in film, except Jack Nicholson he quips. His obsession with film began at age 13.

Darren Linder

Darren grew up in the '70s and has been forever enamored with films from that decade. He is a lifelong resident of Oregon, currently living in Portland. He has performed in many rock bands, ran a non-profit dog rescue, and worked in social service with at-risk youths. Currently he works security in music venues, and is completing a book about his experiences there to be published later this year. His favorite film directors of the '80s are John Carpenter, Brian De Palma and James Cameron.

Stephen Mosley

Stephen is an actor and writer, whose books include 'Christopher Lee: The Loneliness of Evil' (Midnight Marquee Press), 'Klawseye: The Imagination Snatcher of Phantom Island', 'The Lives & Deaths of Morbius Mozella', 'TOWN' and 'The Boy Who Loved Simone Simon'. His film articles have appeared in such magazines as 'Midnight Marquee', 'We Belong Dead' and 'The Dark Side'. His film credits include the evil Ear Goblin in *Kenneth*; the eponymous paranormal investigator of *Kestrel Investigates*; the shady farmer, James, in *Contradiction*; and a blink-and-you'll-miss-it appearance opposite Sam Neill in *Peaky Blinders*. Stephen is one half of the music duo Collinson Twin and lives in a dungeon near Leeds.

Peter Sawford

Peter was born in Essex in 1964 so considers himself a child of the '70s. A self-confessed film buff, he loves watching, reading about and talking about cinema. A frustrated writer his whole life, he's only recently started submitting what he writes to magazines. His favourite director is Alfred Hitchcock with Billy Wilder running him a close second. He still lives in Essex with his wife and works as an IT trainer and when not watching films he's normally panicking over who West Ham are playing next.

Aaron Stielstra

Aaron was born in Ann Arbor, Michigan and grew up in Tucson, AZ and NYC. He is an actor, writer, director, soundtrack composer and illustrator. Since moving to Italy in 2012, he has appeared in spaghetti westerns, numerous crime movies, and horror-thrillers - most of them very wet - and recently completed the punk-rock comedies Weber Falls, USA and Excretion: the Shocking True Story of the Football Mom. He can be seen performing in his band War, Covid & Trump. His favorite '80s actor is Willem Dafoe.

Dr. Andrew C. Webber

Dr. W, a film teacher and examiner for over 35 years, already writes passionately for 'Cinema of the '70s' magazine and also contributes to the cassette gazette fanzine. He pontificates about music on the Low Noise podcast (available on Apple and Spotify) and his blogs can occasionally be found on Oxford's Ultimate Picture Palace cinema website. He still loves being "at" the movies and would describe himself as a lover of cinema, if asked.

Nic Parker

Nic is German but a school trip to Britain sparked her love for that country. She's a true kid of the '80s, stuck in this decade when it comes to music, films and neon colours. She's been a fan of horror since early childhood and is fascinated by all thing creepy and obscure. She has worked as a journalist for German genre magazines 'Moviestar' and 'Deadline' and has also contributed to 'We Belong Dead'. With 'Descent to Hell' her dream to become a novelist came true. She's a sucker for Christmas and lives enslaved by seven cats.

Joseph Secrett

Joseph is a film nut and collector who started at a young age, and quickly became infatuated with all things cinematic. He is a huge fan of 20th century cinema, especially the '60s and '70s for their sheer diversity of genres. Top choices of his include revisionist westerns and seedy crime dramas.

Ian Taylor

Ian dabbled in horror fiction in the early '90s before writing and editing music fanzines. He later adjudicated plays for the Greater Manchester Drama Federation but enjoys film analysis most. Over the last five years, he has become a regular writer and editorial team member for 'We Belong Dead' magazine and contributed to all their book releases. This has led to writing for Dez Skinn's 'Halls of Horror', Allan Bryce's 'Dark Side' and Hemlock's 'Fantastic Fifties', amongst others. His first solo book 'All Sorts of Things Might Happen: The Films of Jenny Agutter' was recently released as a We Belong Dead publication.

Steven West

Steven's first published work was as a floppy haired teenager, voice breaking as he scribbled about Terence Fisher for an early issue of 'We Belong Dead' - a useful break from the lingerie section of the Freeman's catalogue. He still writes for the magazine and its spin offs while regularly contributing to 'The Fantastic Fifties' magazine and the UK Frightfest website, alongside www.horrorscreamsvideovault. co.uk. In 2019, Auteur Publishing released his 'Devil's Advocate' book about Wes Craven's *Scream*. Steven lives in Norfolk with his partner, daughter and - thanks to permanent home working - a dozen sock-puppet 'friends'.

Printed in Great Britain
by Amazon

17212649R00058